PLAGUE IN SURAT
CRISIS IN URBAN GOVERNANCE

INSTITUTE OF SOCIAL SCIENCES
URBAN STUDIES SERIES

1. Urbanisation in Developing Countries: Basic Services and Community Participation
   Edited by **Bidyut Mohanty**

2. Urbanisation in India: Basic Services and People's Participation
   by **K. C. Sivaramakrishnan, Biplab Dasgupta, M. N. Buch**

3. Basic Services for Urban Poor: A Study of Baroda Bhilwara, Sambalpur and Siliguri
   by **Archana Ghosh, S. Sami Ahmad, Shipra Maitra**

4. Urban Poverty, Basic Services and Environment
   by **P. K. Dave, Laurie Baker**

5. Plague in Surat: Crisis in Urban Governance
   by **Archana Ghosh, S. Sami Ahmad**

Urban Studies Series No. 5

Plague in Surat

Crisis in Urban Governance

Archana Ghosh
S. Sami Ahmad

INSTITUTE OF SOCIAL SCIENCES
&
CONCEPT PUBLISHING COMPANY

This study was financially supported by
the Friedrich Ebert Foundation,
India Country Office.

ISBN 81-7022-579-5

First Published 1996

Published by
Ashok Kumar Mittal
Concept Publishing Company
A-15/16 Commercial Block
Mohan Garden
New Delhi 110 059
Phones: 555 4042, 550 4042

Layout by
Institute of Social Sciences
B-7/18 Safdarjung Enclave
New Delhi 110 029

Foreword

THE plague in Surat in September 1994 was a severe jolt to the country's economic progress and urban development. Although, the disease itself was over in a couple of days, even after more than one and a half years, we are yet to overcome the shame it brought to the nation. It has left behind a trail of issues pertaining to our handling of urban governance at the threshold of the 21st century.

The present book is an attempt to identify the factors responsible for the outbreak of plague in Surat. It focusses on three aspects: deterioration of basic amenities in the city, shortcomings of the Surat Municipal Corporation in providing municipal services and the attitude of the councillors towards good governance of the city. This work comprehensively analyses the capabilities of the corporation in solving the civic problems and avoiding a civic crisis in the city. The factors identified in this study represent the typical characteristics of most of the urban local bodies in the country which suffer from acute deficiencies and incompetence. Although this book is focussing on the plague outbreak in Surat, its findings have greater validity for the civic problems our bursting cities are facing all over the country.

The field work for this study was undertaken in Surat when many people were still scared to visit the city. Conducting discussions and interviews with a cross-section of local people, politicians and officials at that juncture was not an easy task. The successful utilisation of data collected from the primary and secondary sources has given this work a distinction of being the first of its kind in the field.

Surat is an example of a city which displays almost all the features of India's urban decay. Look at the figures. Thirty per cent of its population lives in slums, only one-third of its area is covered with sewerage system, drainage is almost absent in major parts of the city and the piles of uncollected garbage is a common sight. While Surat produces nearly 1250 tonnes of refuse everyday, 250 tonnes remain uncollected. Not surprisingly then, Surat has often been referred to as the dirtiest city in India. And not only Surat but India had to pay the price for it dearly.

The entire phenomenon of deteriorating civic condition in Surat is accompanied by a rapid increase in its population. As the second most populous city in Gujarat, Surat accommodates over two million people and for the last three decades it has experienced the highest population growth rate among all the major cities of the state due to migration from other parts of India, especially Orissa, Bihar and Uttar Pradesh. Particularly the last 20 years have been most noticeable in this regard since it was this period which also witnessed the rapid industrialisation in and around the city.

The resultant economic prosperity due to industrial development has also found reflection in the increasing revenue for the Surat Municipal Corporation which is now one of the richest municipal bodies in the country. But still the civic condition in the city, instead of showing any sign of improvement, has only deteriorated over time. It is, therefore, clear that there are variables other than finance which adversely affect local governance of an economically booming city. Collection of huge revenue is one thing. But its proper utilisation for improving the condition of the city is another. Without proper accountability at the political and administrative level, the financial boom could lead to unhygienic and intolerable living conditions. The tragedy of Surat was that the entire system broke down, giving way to corruption, land mafia, speculation and urban underworld in the wake of increased economic possibilities. They could not have thrived without political patronage. The result was that the city government was weak and existed only in form. This theme has rightly been discussed in this book. The basic argument is that effective urban management depends to a greater extent on responsible city government.

The highlight of this book is that it brings out this contradiction – wealth accumulates but city decays – with a great deal of clarity. The study also assesses the role of different governmental and non-governmental organisations in solving the problems of the city in such a situation. It is evident from Surat's example that when the city governments are not doing their job the non-governmental organisations can do precious little because their role is mainly complementary to the corporation or municipality.

Several studies have shown that responsible elected local bodies with adequate powers can act as an effective early warning system to prevent calamities, epidemics and social disorders. James Manor's study of panchayati raj in Karnataka shows that these institutions are not only a foolproof source of early warnings about potential calamities, but also an effective means of ensuring that such warnings do not go unheeded. Based on his study, in a paper published in *Economic and Political Weekly* (May 22, 1993), Manor stated that although a free press had a vital role in this regard, the journalists in Karnataka themselves had asserted that "strong panchayati raj institutions of the kind that existed in Karnataka between 1987 and 1991 provided a far more reliable source of early warnings than journalists could".

However, the elected bodies alone are not the guarantee against the urban degeneration. The elected representatives can be highly irresponsible when they are embroiled in politicking for their own survival. Drawing lessons from the Karnataka experience, it is possible to hypothesise that there are three pre-conditions which make a local government effective in addressing the crying problems of the people. First, democratically elected local government institutions must not be weak. Secondly, elected members must have powers over bureaucrats to prompt them for action. And thirdly, there must be a strong presence of opposition party representatives so that if the ruling party members are lethargic to act, the opposition can hound them.

In all the above mentioned aspects the local government in Surat was found wanting. The civic condition in the city deteriorated during a phase when the municipal corporation had an elected body. This book tells us that even in the duly elected local body there had been frequent shifts in power from one party to the other, leading to uncertainty, confusion and instability in the activities of the corporation. The period 1981-90 is particularly important because it witnessed the exchange of power as many as eight times between the BJP and the Congress. In fact, during this period the the power shift from party to party was so frequent that no party had a tenure for more than two years. And in such a situation of flux the opposition carried only limited weight when change in political allegiance and horse-trading was the order of the day. Besides, the councillors had little control over the commissioner who is directly accountable to the government.

It is time we change the predominant position of commissioners in municipalities and corporations. All municipal corporations in the country had adopted the "Bombay model" – the Bombay Municipal Corporation Act 1888 under which a state-appointed official – the Commissioner – functioned as a co-ordinating authority along with the council and its standing committee. All the three derived executive power from the legislation itself. This was an anomaly. Another contradiction was that the Commissioner was responsible for implementing the decisions of the council and its standing committee. The Calcutta and Howrah municipal corporations were the first two to move against this system in 1980 opting for a Mayor-in-Council system which is in tune with the cabinet system of government. It has been found that Mayor-in-Council system in Calcutta and Howrah are more efficient and effective than the Commissioner system. In the wake of Constitution (74th Amendment) Act there is a general move for adopting Mayor-in-Council system throughout the country. If that happens, chances of 'Surat 1994' repeating itself will be less.

The plague outbreak was the second major calamity in

Surat within a short span of two years. The first was the communal riot in the wake of developments in Ayodhya in December 1992. Both these calamities were man-made and could have been avoided if only Surat had a responsible and strong local government.

Surat's problem is not an isolated phenomenon. In fact, in the face of the civic mess and urban disorder, most of the cities in India are sitting on a volcano. Therefore, the findings of this book have a greater relevance and a wider applicability. It is being published at a time when we are in the process of implementing the Constitution (74th Amendment) Act. Undoubtedly, people have high expectations and they believe that the new system will bring a remarkable improvement in the governance of their cities and towns, making them more liveable. The provision of reservations in the Act for the deprived sections such as SC/ST and 33 per cent seats for women has further enhanced people's aspirations. But it must be remembered that constitutional provision is not an end in itself. What is actually required is a more realistic perception of, and the active efforts for, solving the civic problems of our cities on the part of elected representatives, officials and the people. These are synonymous with what is commonly called 'civic conscience'. It connotes awareness and understanding of one's rights and obligations as a member of a large community.

Let us hope that with the implementation of the Constitution (74th Amendment) Act and the Conformity Acts in all the states, the probability of our cities and towns degenerating to the level of 'Surat 1994' will be far remote. Besides being a useful contribution to the literature on urban studies, this book, which is the fifth in the urban studies series of the Institute of Social Sciences, will be a useful reader for elected corporators, councillors as well as government officials in their task of making urban centres liveable and sustainable.

March 31, 1996

George Mathew
Director

Acknowledgements

THIS study was made possible due to active cooperation of several friends, well-wishers and institutions. We would particularly like to acknowledge the support of the then Administrator Mr. P. K. Ghosh and the Commissioner Mr. Balwant Singh of the Surat Municipal Corporation who patiently discussed with us various issues pertaining to the system of governance in Surat. Besides, other departmental heads of the corporation, senior officials of the Bank of Baroda in Surat and the Surat Urban Development Authority were very helpful in providing data and source materials. We are thankful to all of them.

We wish to thank Prof. Ghanshyam Shah, Director, Centre for Social Studies, Surat, the President and other office-bearers of the Southern Gujarat Chamber of Commerce and Industry for their valuable assistance and to a large number of ex-corporators, NGOs, trade union leaders and press persons in Surat for responding to our queries in the process of gathering information.

Dr. Heinz Bongartz, Resident Representative, Friedrich Ebert Foundation (FEF) and a friend of the Institute of Social Sciences, extended his unreserved support for this study. We acknowledge with gratitude his interest in and the FEF support for the Urban Studies Department of the Institute of Social Sciences. We also express our sincere gratitude to Prof. M. A. Oommen, Senior Fellow at the Institute, for taking a keen interest in this study and offering his valuable suggestions. Our special thanks are due to Dr. Shipra Maitra, our former colleague, who helped us in the field survey and wrote sections of the draft report.

Mr. C. L. Master and Ms. Pervin M. Dordi of Surat Municipal Corporation deserve special mention for extending help during our stay in Surat for the field work.

Our thanks are also due to Ms Suhasini Ramaswamy for her editorial assistance. We greatly appreciate the support of Mr. P. Nandakumar for doing the word processing, Mr. P. N. Kuttappan for the layout.

Archana Ghosh
S. Sami Ahmad

Contents

List of Tables

CHAPTER I

Introduction

THE suspected plague epidemic which started in Beed district of Maharashtra in the first week of September 1994 spread rapidly and affected the city of Surat on September 20. By September end, official records confirmed that there were 1300 plague patients, though the casualty figures were limited to 70. There was a serious doubt prevailing in the minds of civic officials, health workers and medical research fraternity whether the disease which struck Surat was really plague or not. But putting an end to all the controversies the committee set up by the Government of India late 1994 confirmed in early February 1995 that the disease in Surat was truly pneumonic plague caused by the safety-pin shaped organism called *Yersinia Pestis*.

The reappearance of plague which was last reported in the country in 1966 in Kolar district of Karnataka not only created widespread panic and put a severe blow to Surat's economy but had much wider repercussions on the economy of the country as a whole including industrial production, tourism, export etc. The rough estimates put the loss to industry in Surat in several crores of rupees. During the peak period of the epidemic a total of Rs. 25 crores was suffered on a daily basis by the textile industries. The diamond cutting and polishing industry was losing Rs. 16 crores every day. Plastic, zari and engineering industries together incurred a loss of Rs. 3.85 crores per day. On the export front the loss was nearly Rs. 2 crores. Moreover the Surat Municipal Corporation (SMC) lost about Rs. 25 lakhs in octroi collection every day.

It had also its international ramification. India's image before the world faced a severe blow. The exaggerated news spread by the Indian media was picked up by the foreign press in no time. The stories circulated by foreign press, especially the BBC, highlighted the insanitary conditions in the affected areas, breakdown of health services, law and order problems and administrative negligence. The foreign media projected India as a primitive rat-worshipping society, steeped in superstition. Foreign investors were cautioned to think twice before plunging into huge investments in India. Some of the foreign airlines temporarily stopped their flights to and from India, and some countries banned import of food from here and quarantined passengers from India for exhaustive medical check-ups.

The intensity of the disease subsided by the early October 1994. Both the Government of India and WHO certified Surat as 'plague-free'. In fact, WHO certified India's commendable performance in controlling the disease in such a short period.

The entire episode, however, has raised certain vital questions. The most important among them are the questions related to urban governance in Surat and for that matter in the country as a whole. The occurrence of plague at the advent of the twenty-first century represents the sorry state of the country's lopsided urban growth, poor basic services and lacunae in the entire urban management and administration.

The metros and megapolises in the developing countries pose a typical case of urban environmental decay which can be explained in terms of "population pressure together with direct and indirect institutional weaknesses which leads to urban growth over and above the carrying capacity of a city's natural and living environment, causing congestion of urban infrastructure and environmental degradation" (Shin 1994). Indian cities are no exceptions.

The Jagmohan Committee which was constituted to advise the state government of Delhi in the wake of the plague scare, in its recently brought out report states that the capital city suffers from acute shortage of drinking water, solid waste disposal facilities and excessively high level of air and water pollution which have led to an increase in the incidence of serious diseases like tuberculosis, bronchitis, asthma, etc. The report comments that this, besides putting an unbearable pressure on the health services, is lowering the overall productivity of the city and turning it into a "Dickensian hell of haze, smoke and urban blight".

The cities do not have any disease surveillance system either. Dr. K. K. Datta, Director, National Institute of Communicable Diseases expressed that, "Diseases like plague and malaria give early warning signals. We should recognise those signals and learn to respond to them with appropriate action. Unfortunately our health system does not tap the signals and when it does take action, it is further disadvantaged by the machinery which is not effective enough *(Indian Express,* 25 December 1994).

Surat which is described as one big 'transit camp' of migrant workers from different parts of the country could not cope with the exorbitant growth in population. Its population increased more than three times from 4.93 lakhs to 15.17 lakhs during 1971 to 1991. Though the city's economic activity has increased manifold through unprecedented growth of small scale industries in the unorganized sector and the setting up of some large industries by big industrial houses, people's living conditions have deteriorated to such an extent that Surat is said to be the dirtiest city of its size in the whole country. The development of basic amenities has lagged far behind the growth in the city's population. The social milieu of the city has also changed because of unwarranted and unplanned growth. The builders and promoters of real estate in the city and its periphery have created a law and order problem. Gangsters, bootleggers and land mafia have become all powerful in the city. The outbreak of plague in Surat may be the culmination of all these factors.

Even then it is the alert and conscious city government which is quick to respond that makes all the difference between success and disaster in the management of an urban crisis. Like Surat, Bombay, the largest metropolis of the country, and Delhi, the capital city, also faced a similar threat of plague. While the administration in Delhi overreacted to the situation by closing all its schools and colleges, Bombay responded with resilience and efficiency. The civic administration moved swiftly to clean up the city, launched a shanty to shanty survey for plague cases and covered five to six million people in four days through its network of 176 health posts. It also swiftly set up monitoring posts at railway and bus stations to screen incoming passengers from Surat (Fernandes 1994).

In the case of Surat grave misgivings were expressed about the way the state government and the city government handled the situation arising out of the plague outbreak which led to an exodus of more than six lakh people from the city. This tragedy happened at a time when there was no democratically elected local government in the city for quite some time. Though the term of the previous elected body in the corporation ended in 1992 elections were postponed more than once on various pretexts.

Against the backdrop of the preceding discussion the present study was undertaken in October 1994 immediately after the outbreak of the plague in Surat. By taking the case of Surat it intends to draw some general conclusions regarding the problems of urban governance in the country's rapidly growing metros.

Focus of the Study

1. Is it correct to assume that the Surat tragedy happened because of the absence of an elected local government?
2. Did it occur because the city administration was not doing its work in spite of the fact that Surat had an elected corporation since 1966?
3. If they were indifferent or not doing their duty, what were the reasons?
4. If our concern is for elected city governments, what are the prerequisites for their effective functioning?

Objective of the Study

The present study is an attempt to analyse the factors leading to the deterioration of the basic amenities and consequent outbreak of the plague epidemic in Surat and in that perspective the functioning of the city government in the past and present. The study is based on the premise that effective urban management depends to a great extent on a strong city government which means:

i) democratically elected representatives manage the city affairs,
ii) the elected local government has sufficient power to take necessary action for the safety and well-being of its citizens, and
iii) there are strong forces to maintain proper checks and balances within and outside the city government.

Methodology and Data Source

The study is primarily based on field survey conducted in Surat in December 1994. Data were collected from various sources which include:

(i) published and unpublished reports, documents etc.,
ii) direct interviews with a cross-section of the people,
iii) questionnaire survey through partly structured schedules, and
iv) observation by researchers.

The respondents of the direct interview constitute the representative samples of the following groups:

i) Former corporators of Surat Municipal Corporation,
ii) Officials of the corporation and other authorities which are responsible for the provision of basic amenities in the city,
iii) Representatives of industries,

iv) Prominent citizens,
v) The leaders of the recognized trade unions,
vi) NGO representatives,
vii) Local media, and
viii) Common people.

In the process we got opinions from 15 ex-corporators either through direct interviews or questionnaire survey. The Administrator, Commissioner and all senior officials of the Surat Municipal Corporation and senior executives of Surat Urban Development Authority, prominent academicians, senior citizens, president and senior executives of the Southern Gujarat Chamber of Commerce and Industry, senior officials of the Bank of Baroda, leaders of important workers' unions, editors of local newspapers were interviewed directly by the members of the research team. We also got the views of eight prominent NGO representatives through partly structured questionnaires.

To have an overview of the living conditions of the poor and to get their opinions about the civic amenities we visited slums in different parts of the city especially in those areas which were affected by the recent flood and plague. The information gathered through these direct and indirect interviews and the secondary source materials we collected from different sources form the basis of the present study.

The draft report of the study was discussed at a seminar in Surat on 8 April 1995. A select group of academicians, officials, politicians and NGOs, mostly from Surat, gave their views on the findings of the study. While finalising the report their suggestions and comments were carefully considered and necessary incorporations and modifications were made.

The book is divided into five chapters. The second chapter following this introductory one gives a profile of the city which contains the historical evolution, demographic trends, present industrial scenario and the organisational set-up for administration and management of civic affairs. The third chapter gives an overview of the condition of important basic amenities in the city and their impact on the quality of life. The fourth chapter is an assessment of the functioning of the city government, its problems and people's responses towards it. The final chapter gives the conclusion and projects some future strategies which emerged during our discussion with different respondent groups.

CHAPTER II

City Profile

1. Historical Evolution of the City and its Regional Significance

THE transition of Surat city from a small trading centre to a sprawling metropolis has been a complex process spread over several hundred years. The evolution of the city has taken shape through changes in economic profiles, administrative structure, physical boundaries and demographic composition.

The modern city of Surat which has a glorious history dating back to 300 B.C. owes its name to the old Hindu town of Suryapur. Administratively the Gujarat region including the city of Surat has undergone a significant change over time. It was under the power of Hindu rulers up to 1194. After intermittent rules by various Hindu dynasties and several Muslim invasions the region finally came under the Muslim rulers in the last part of the sixteenth century. During the Mughal rule especially during Akbar's regime the city acquired its glory as a prominent trade centre and a port city. Under subsequent rulers during the Mughal period the city expanded in area and population. Its appearance also improved because prominent buildings and market places were constructed by the rulers. The town during this period was moderately large and well-built.

However, with the gradual decline of the Mughal empire as the trading and commercial activity of the British increased, their administrative interests also spread in the region. In 1759 the British took administrative charge of the city and it further expanded in area and population. By the beginning of the twentieth century it became well connected by rail, roads and bridges with the surrounding areas and with other important cities in the country.

Because of its important location on the river Tapi (local

name of the Tapti river) and having a coastal belt of around 6 km. along the Arabian Sea on the western part of the city, it came to prominence as an important trading centre in the latter part of the fifteenth century. After the decline in the prosperity of Rander (another important port city in western Gujarat) because of frequent raids by the Portuguese, Surat became the most important trade link between India and many other countries.

Before 1759 when the British took over the administrative charge of the city it had already established contacts with merchants from other European countries like Portugal, Netherlands and France. The English began their trade with Surat in 1608. Even prior to that during Akbar's time this region was known as the Emporium of Trades. The port city of Surat was actually the creation of the Mughals. Till the rise of Bombay port in the seventeenth and eighteenth centuries Surat was at the height of prosperity (Government of Gujarat 1991). The Arab, Turk, Iranian and Jewish traders settled in the town of Surat and Khambat which enjoyed the status of international ports. These traders had brisk business with neighbouring countries like Java, Sumatra, Malaya, Burma, Sri Lanka, the Persian Gulf countries, Red Sea ports and other far flung areas. Also it had trade links with prominent cities all over India like Golconda, Burhanpur, Lahore, Ahmedabad, Agra and Delhi.

The city was famous not only for its trading activities. Surat became famous for its manufacturing activities as well. Surat was a flourishing centre for ship building activities. The East India Company not only got its ships repaired from Surat Dockyard but also got ships built at Surat along with Navsari and Gandhi. Even the Dutch and French used to get their warships made at Surat. The whole coast of Tapi from Athwa lines to Dumas was specially meant for ship builders, who were usually Parsis. They engaged nearly 7000 to 8000 workers who were usually Hindus (Government of Gujarat 1991).

Though the ships built here were imitations of British ships, the Surat ship builders were acquainted with the Chinese and Arabian types as well and often built such ships. With the decline of the port of Surat after the rise of Bombay port the ship building industry also faced a severe blow. The strong resistance from the ship builders in England and introduction of speedy steamships added a further blow to the industry.

After the decline of the ship building industry in the early nineteenth century the other major industry which flourished and provided employment to the majority of the population was cotton textile industry. However big industrial establishments were rare phenomena in Surat. Except for three big cotton mills all the other enterprises were small family based handloom units. The other important additions to the industrial scenario were zari and kimkhab making units. These were also small scale units usually managed at the household level.

However unlike zari and kimkhab industries which had very limited market potentials, the weaving industry cut a niche of its own. The evolution of the powerloom and handloom expanded the scope of tremendous activities in this sector. Since Independence the number of looms and people employed in this sector has increased at a tremendous pace.

In keeping with the growth in textile industries some auxiliary activities started gradually. Engineering units producing machinery for zari, silk and artsilk industries and other related machines also came up. Another important addition to the industrial activity of the city since the 1950s is the diamond cutting and polishing industry. Barring a few big units which have recently come up, diamond cutting and processing was also confined to small enterprises. Even now a majority of the diamond processing units are in the small sector.

The last two decades especially the eighties observed a vast change in the industrial activities in Surat and its peripheries. Many big industries have come up in and around the city and the importance of Surat in the regional context has increased manifold. The regional importance of the city along with Baroda and Ahmedabad has grown tremendously in the recent decades because of its specific location at the core of what is called the "Golden Corridor" of industrial development. The corridor some 450 kms long and 40 kms wide, extends from Vapi in the south of Surat to Mehsana to the north of Ahmedabad. Immediately after the city limit in the Hajira belt the industries like petrochemicals, steel, cement, fertilizer, power, structural fabrication, oil and liquid petroleum have come up involving total investment of nearly Rs. 27,000 crores, one-third of which has already been invested during the last few years. The findings of oil and natural gas along the corridor in Bharuch and Ankleswar has further enhanced its importance. The development of Ankleswar Industrial Estate in the north and Vapi Industrial Estate in the south has brought tremendous economic prosperity to the city. In the southern part of the city there are the industrial complexes of Gujarat Industrial Development Corporation, Sachin and Diamond Nagar. There are sugar, paper, textile industries in the northern border of the city.

Besides industrial potential the city has fertile agricultural land irrigated by intensive canal network. The combined effect of all these on the economic prosperity of the city has been remarkable. The sudden spurt in economic activities in the city and its outskirts has changed the otherwise small and quiet town into a humming metropolis.

Over the years the expansion of the physical boundaries of the city has been enormous. From 1.78 sq. km. in 1664 the city has expanded to 111.16 sq. km in 1986. The city before 1986 included the walled city and surrounding areas expanded in all directions. Development took place along the road and railway lines connecting Amroli and Ahmedabad in the north, Kamrej road and Bardoli road in the east, Udhna road in the south, Udhna Magdalla road and Dumas road in the south-west and Rander road in the west (SUDA 1980). After the expansion in 1986, the city extended further mainly in the south and south-east. The city is divided by the river Tapi. The western part of the city which includes Jahangirpura, Jahangirabad, Rander, Adajan etc is connected by bridges with the eastern part.

2. Demographic Profile

Surat is India's twelfth and Gujarat's second most populous city. Located in the southern part of Gujarat it is one of the 11 cities spread across the country which became a metropolis in 1991 by crossing the one million population mark (Census of India 1991a). Currently its population is estimated to be around two million. Surat has attained this figure by experiencing a very rapid population growth in a period of just 20 years. This rapid population increase in a very short time span is actually the hallmark of Surat's demographic trends. During the decade 1971-81 its growth rate was 85.35 per cent which was the highest among all the present day metropolises, while the decade 1981-91 once again witnessed a remarkably high growth rate of over 66 percent in the city which was next only to Vishakhapatnam (74.26%) and Hyderabad (68.12%) in the same category of cities.

At the state level, as Table 3 reveals, Surat has the largest population after Ahmedabad, the capital city of the state. However, a look at the population growth trends of six major cities of the state indicates that during all the three census decades of 1961-71, 1971-81 and 1981-91 Surat experienced the highest population growth rates (Table 4).

Table 4 further shows that similar to the trend in the all India urban population growth, all the six major cities of the state have seen a decline in the population growth rates between the two decades of 1971-81 and 1981-91. However, it is important to point out that as far as Surat's declining population growth trend during the 1981-91 is concerned, it was the result of an economic and industrial recession of the city during the late 1980s which not only caused a relatively low flow of migrants to the city but also forced people to outmigrate temporarily. Tentative estimates showed that there was a net loss of almost one lakh people in the city when the census took place in 1991. If this factor is taken into account the growth rate of Surat population during 1981-91 would be much more than what has been indicated in the 1991 census.

TABLE 1
Metropolitan Cities in 1991 Arranged in Descending Order of their Population

(*in million*)

City	1961	1971	1981	1991
Greater Bombay	4.15	5.97	8.24	12.57
Calcutta	5.98	7.42	9.19	10.91
Delhi	2.35	3.64	5.72	8.37
Madras	1.94	3.16	4.28	5.36
Hyderabad	1.24	1.79	2.54	4.28
Bangalore	1.20	1.66	2.92	4.08
Ahmedabad	1.20	1.75	2.54	3.29
Pune	0.79	1.13	1.68	2.48
Kanpur	0.97	1.27	1.63	2.11
Nagpur	0.69	0.93	1.30	1.66
Lucknow	0.65	0.81	1.00	1.64
Surat	0.31	0.49	0.91	1.51
Jaipur	0.41	0.63	1.01	1.51
Kochi	0.29	0.50	0.68	1.13
Coimbatore	0.44	0.73	0.92	1.13
Vadodara	0.30	0.46	0.74	1.11
Indore	0.39	0.56	0.82	1.10
Patna	0.41	0.55	0.91	1.09
Madurai	0.49	0.71	0.90	1.09
Bhopal	0.22	0.38	0.67	1.06
Vishakhapatnam	0.21	0.36	0.60	1.05
Varanasi	0.50	0.63	0.79	1.02
Ludhiana	0.24	0.40	0.60	1.01

Source: Census of India 1991a.

TABLE 2
Decadal Growth Rates of Metropolitan Cities in India: 1961 - 1991

(*in percentage*)

City	1961-71	1971-81	1981-91
Greater Bombay	43.80	38.06	52.50
Calcutta	24.0	23.90	18.73
Delhi	54.57	57.09	46.18
Madras	63.02	35.31	25.0
Hyderabad	43.80	41.72	68.12
Bangalore	37.88	75.56	39.86
Ahmedabad	45.30	45.40	29.41
Pune	43.53	48.55	47.38
Kanpur	31.32	28.52	28.81
Nagpur	34.79	39.93	27.59
Lucknow	24.14	23.78	62.97
Surat	55.26	85.35	66.01
Jaipur	55.16	59.42	49.18
Kochi	73.13	35.58	66.15
Coimbatore	64.25	25.01	23.38
Vadodara	50.94	59.33	49.72
Indore	42.03	47.84	33.12
Patna	32.88	66.70	19.55
Madurai	44.94	27.57	29.48
Bhopal	72.62	74.35	58.51
Vishakhapatnam	72.10	66.07	74.26
Varanasi	25.54	25.50	28.76
Ludhiana	64.40	51.31	66.71

Remarkably, the decline in the growth rate of Surat's population between 1971-81 and 1981-91 had been accompanied by the areal expansion of the city's boundary which was doubled from 55.60 sq. km to 111.16 sq. km in 1986 covering mainly the peripheral areas in the southern and the eastern outskirts of the city (Table 5).

TABLE 3
Population of Six Major Cities in Gujarat: 1961-1991

(*in million*)

City	1961	1971	1981	1991
Ahmedabad	1.20	1.75	2.54	3.29
Bhavnagar	0.17	0.22	0.30	0.40
Jamnagar	0.15	0.22	0.31	0.36
Rajkot	0.19	0.30	0.44	0.65
Surat	0.31	0.49	0.91	1.51
Vadodara	0.30	0.46	0.74	1.11

Sources: Census of India 1981; Census of India 1991a.

TABLE 4
Decadal Growth Rates in Six Major Cities in Gujarat: 1961-1991

(*in percentage*)

City	Growth rate		
	1961-71	1971-81	1981-91
Ahmedabad	45.30	45.40	29.41
Bhavnagar	28.05	36.58	30.74
Jamnagar	42.97	39.41	15.16
Rajkot	54.84	48.06	46.27
Surat	55.27	85.35	66.01
Vadodara	50.94	59.33	49.72

Sources: Based on Census of India, 1981; Census of India 1991a.

TABLE 5
Areal Expansion of Surat

Year	Increase in area (sq. km.)	Total area of the city (sq. km.)
Before 1963	-	8.18
1963	13.77	21.95
1970	11.85	33.80
1975	21.75	55.55
1986	55.60	111.16

Source: Mehta, 1989.

In fact, the interplay between the areal expansion and population growth in Surat has over time caused a shift in the proportional distribution of population in different parts of the city. Table 6 reveals the population, proportion and density in Surat on areal basis during 1961-91.

Table 6 further shows that although in the inner or old city the population has consistently increased, the density has shown a marginal decline in the last decade resulting in a corresponding increase in density in the inner periphery. This indicates that because of extreme congestion and high land value in the core city more and more people are concentrating in peripheral areas. In the process, Rander Zone in the western part of the city seems to be the major target of population concentration where during 1981-91 the population and density both have roughly doubled. Nevertheless, the population proportion remained the same between 1981 and 1991 at 43 percent because of the addition of outer periphery in the 1991 census which now accommodates 29 percent of the city's population.

TABLE 6

Distribution of Population and Density in Different Zones in Surat: 1971 - 1991

	1971			1981			1991		
	Population	(%)	Density	Population	(%)	Density	Population	(%)	Density
Inner or old city zone	3,63,703	77	44,462	4,41,325	57	53,952	4,24,353	28	51,876
Inner periphery and Rander Zone	1,07,953	23	4,214	3,35,258	43	7,076	6,44,152	43	13,598
Outer periphery	-	-	-	-	-	-	4,30,312	29	7,739
All Surat	4,71,656	100	13,954	7,76,583	100	13,977	14,98,817	100	14,818

Source: Das, 1994.

A significant contributor to the city's spectacular population increase is the phenomenal migration of people from different parts of the country, particularly from Uttar Pradesh, Bihar, Maharashtra and other parts of Gujarat who get attracted to this city because of its industrial advancement. The growth of industrial production has been on a substantial scale by means of small industry carried on in workshops, rough sheds and households. The industries that are either wholly or partly in the small or less regulated or informal sector are textiles including the production of artificial silk (Surat produces 60% of India's artificial silk) and zari industries, textile processing and the production of parts of textile and garment making, diamond cutting and polishing (30% of India's turnover in this sector is from Surat), plastics, engineering, and chemicals and dyes. There has also been growth in the high investment organized sector, notably chemicals and petrochemicals, and in the financial sector and the transport sector (Ramachandran, 1994).

An extremely high job potential in Surat emanating from its flourishing industrial base has resulted in 57.60 percent male work force participation rate which is the highest in all the six big cities in Gujarat (Table 7).

TABLE 7

Work Force Participation Rates in Six Major Cities in Gujarat: 1981-1991

(*in percentage*)

City	1981			1991		
	Total	Male	Female	Total	Male	Female
Gujarat (Urban)	28.77	49.84	5.5	29.50	50.85	6.02
Ahmedabad	28.8	49.64	4.65	28.95	49.73	5.58
Bhavnagar	26.88	48.07	3.96	27.80	49.13	4.76
Jamnagar	28.84	50.67	5.01	29.62	52.01	5.26
Rajkot	27.28	48.94	3.87	29.46	51.81	5.27
Surat	34.27	57.37	6.78	34.00	57.60	5.88
Vadodara	29.13	50.23	5.41	29.76	50.45	6.72

Sources: Census of India 1981; Census of India 1991c.
Note: Table includes main workers only.

As far as female work force participation rate is concerned Surat occupies the second place after Vadodara. Although the country's socio-economic fabric does not permit large scale female participation in economic activities, particularly those pertaining to urban based secondary and tertiary sectors, this is more so in Surat where the economic infrastructure has largely been detrimental to any significant female participation in the work force. Their participation is negligible in the diamond industry and very limited in textile industries where powerlooms are already replacing traditional weaving which had a higher scope for women. Similar is the case with a host of other newly emerging modern industries in the city.

The distribution of these workers in four broad categories of economic activities indicates that a major concentration of the work force is in the 'other' workers category comprising trade and commerce and non-household industries. Other economic activities shared only 5.06 percent of the work force in 1991. As Table 8 indicates, in the categories of cultivators and agricultural labourers their proportion is even less than 1 percent. Obviously, the strong secondary and tertiary sectors dominated economic base of the city does not encourage these primary sector activities.

In a comparative perspective of the work force structure of major cities in Gujarat it is clear that in Surat there has been a gradual increase in the proportion of workers in 'other workers' categories. This is in total contrast to the trend in most of the other major cities of Gujarat where the proportion of such workers has declined over time.

A typical impact of the economic and industrial character of the city may also be seen in a very low sex ratio in the city. In fact with only 839 females per thousand males Surat has the lowest sex ratio among all the six major cities of the state. As Table 9 shows, since 1961 the city has been consistently experiencing a decline in the sex ratio as it moved from 921 in

TABLE 8

Distribution of Main Workers in Six Major Cities of Gujarat: 1971-91

(*in percentage*)

State/City	Cultivators			Agricultural labourers			Workers in household industry			Other workers		
	1971	1981	1991	1971	1981	1991	1971	1981	1991	1971	1981	1991
Gujarat (Urban)	5.43	3.98	3.43	4.55	4.53	4.66	3.00	2.75	2.63	87.02	88.74	89.28
Ahmedabad	.30	.34	.58	.14	0.51	.50	1.55	2.08	2.44	98.01	97.07	96.48
Bhavnagar	.67	0.66	0.57	.83	0.39	0.87	1.21	2.45	1.79	97.29	96.50	96.77
Jamnagar	2.27	1.99	1.37	1.25	1.57	0.61	1.70	2.24	2.15	94.78	94.20	95.87
Rajkot	1.50	-	1.69	.48	-	2.34	1.35	-	3.28	96.67	-	92.69
Surat	.70	0.65	0.49	2.70	1.53	0.90	7.03	4.95	3.67	89.57	92.87	94.94
Vadodara	1.44	1.27	1.20	1.23	1.70	1.45	1.36	1.42	1.59	95.97	95.67	95.76

Sources: Census of India 1971; Census of India 1981; Census of India 1991b.

1961 to 839 in 1991. No other major city in the state had experienced such a drastic decline in the sex ratio during the same period. Whereas in Ahmedabad, Vadodara, Bhavnagar and Jamnagar it actually increased, albeit a little, the decline in Rajkot was very insignificant.

TABLE 9
Sex Ratio in Six Major Cities of Gujarat: 1961-1991

City	1961	1971	1981	1991
Ahmedabad	804	830	869	896
Bhavnagar	916	908	925	929
Jamnagar	907	913	916	936
Rajkot	927	920	925	925
Surat	921	884	840	839
Vadodara	856	852	889	898

Sources: Census of India 1971; Census of India 1991a.

The declining sex ratio in Surat is mainly attributed to the growing industrialization in the city during the 1960s and 1970s which resulted in a large number of migrant workers from different parts of the country working in various industries who generally come alone, leaving behind their families back at home. In many cases even if the migrants come with their families they remain male dominated ones and contribute further to the deterioration of the sex ratio in the city.

3. Economic Profile

Present Industrial Scenario

The economic development of Surat, as has been indicated earlier, dates back to the thirteenth century when it was a very important port on the banks of the river Tapi. It has experienced various changes in economic characteristics since then. In the 1961 census, it was classified under "Manufacturing with moderate service and low trade and transport". Though manufacturing is still the most important sector, the role of the service industry has increased tremendously over time. Now it is the most dominant economic unit in the whole district of Surat.

The national policy of providing various incentives to the small scale industrial sector led to the rapid industrialization of Surat in the post-Independence era. The city of Surat was experiencing major growth in small scale industry (specially in synthetic fibre). The various incentives to small scale industries offered by the state government during the late fifties resulted in a mushroom growth of powerloom based textile industries in the expanded municipal boundary during the 1960s. The bank nationalization of 1969 opened up an easier source of finance in this sector. Industrial establishments like Udhna Udyog Nagar and others in Katargam, Sachin and Pandesara developed in the then peripheral area of the city boundary. The diamond and zari industries also experienced substantial growth during the 1960s and 1970s as most of these industries are in the small scale sector. With the expansion of the city area in 1970 and 1975, a number of such small industrial units in surrounding rural areas came under the corporation administration. In 1986, the city area almost doubled, with major expansion towards the south, which experienced substantial industrial activities.

The unprecedented growth of small scale industries in the unorganized sector since the 1960s, added significantly to its population. According to the 1971 census, 83.5 percent of all industrial units in the district were in Surat city, providing 71.3 percent of total industrial employment in the district. The phenomenal industrial development during the last two decades was also primarily concentrated in Surat city and its neighbouring areas, namely Udhna, Pandesara, Bardoli, Vyara etc. Large scale industries have accelerated the population growth rate since the mid eighties.

Major and medium industrial activities are located in the northern and southern parts of the SMC area, mostly along both the sides of the trunk railway line linking Surat with Bombay and Ahmedabad. Three big industrial estates, one in the north (Katargam), another in the south-west (Katodra) and the third in the extreme south (Pandesara) as well as the mini industrial estates of diamond cutting and polishing in the eastern corridor (Nana-Varachha Road) are the major industrial establishments in the SMC territory outside the walled city area.

Among the major industries in Surat, therefore, diamond cutting, textile, zari, dyeing and printing, initially flourished as either small scale or household industries. Diamond is an export based industry while textile, zari and others primarily cater to the domestic market. In fact, the city is a major producing centre for synthetic fabrics and zari in India. The finest quality of art silk and cotton fabrics are produced in Surat. The handlooms have been fast converted into power looms.

Besides these industries, which are basically small scale ones, the Gujarat Industrial Development Corporation has established five industrial estates in the district, three of which have been in and around Surat city. Textiles, engineering goods and fertilizers are the dominant large scale industries here.

Surat has the distinction of having the pioneer co-operative industrial estate in the country. Udhna Co-operative Industrial Estate is established with approximately 500 units, a majority belonging to the textile group, followed by engineering and chemicals.

The industries in Surat have been dominantly characterized by small scale manufacturing and allied activities. The city economy mainly depended on zari and art silk industries which were primarily home-based, the artisans migrating from the surrounding hinterland. Diamond cutting and its polishing become another major activity in the city at a much later period. A majority of the activities in these industries, however, remain within the unorganized sector and subdivided under names within the family, in order to avoid the Factory Act, 1948. This is corroborated by Table 10 showing less than one percent of the small scale industries as registered. The number of small scale industries registered under the Factory Act is almost negligible.

TABLE 10

Industrial Establishments in Surat: 1994

Sl. No.	Classification	Number
1.	Large-scale	88
2.	Small-scale industries	19763
3.	Registered small-scale industries	89
4.	Registered under Factories Act	8

Sources: Annual Credit Plan, 1994-95; Bank of Baroda (Surat).

Note: The Directorate of Factories covers units under Indian Factories Act, i.e, industrial units employing either 10 or more persons with power operated machines or 20 or more persons without power operated machines. The District Industries Office keeps record of those units which are only registered with their office. This registration is done by only those units which are interested in getting financial assistance.

The unorganized sector dominates the industrial scenario in Surat. These small scale units are owned by self-employed local weavers. But a sizable proportion are fabricated by the owners to circumvent the rules of the Factory Act, with fictitious sub-division of ownership and management within the family.

Employment in Industries

The employment situation in Surat is very casual in nature. Employment figures in the unorganized sector are kept low in order to avoid labour laws. The workers do not earn fixed wages. Employment is temporary and wages are based on productivity. They do not have earned holidays or fixed working hours. A majority of the workers have a per-capita monthly income of less than Rs. 1000, while 36 to 38 percent of them earn between Rs. 1000 and Rs. 1500. They are under constant threat of insecurity, with very little bargaining power, worsened by a continuous flow of immigrants. There are some trade union activities among textile workers. It may be observed that a majority of the textile units are registered (Table 11). In the diamond industry, such activities are non-existent. The labourers are generally hired through the contract labour system. The contractor is responsible for the quantity and quality of the labour force. He often shifts labourers from one unit to another. The floating nature of the labour force dampens the possibility of any strong trade-union organization. A majority of the workers remain unemployed for some days every month. The study by South Gujarat University (1984) has shown that less than 20 percent of the workers are continuing in their present job for over two years. Many workers have strong village connections, where they go back in the harvest season (Kashyap and Tiwari 1986). However, the wage-level in the city, though not high, is sufficient to keep them tied to the city with continuous search for opportunities to earn more.

TABLE 11

Percentage Distribution of Industrial Establishments in Surat under Different Categories

Industry	Factory sector	Non-factory sector	
		Registered	Unregistered
Art silk	20	55	25
Diamond	15	35	50
Others	10	30	60

Sources: State Bureau of Economics & Statistics, Ahmedabad; Inspectorate of Factories, Surat.

Low level of earning however, does not always direct the workers to reside in slums. Social and cultural bondage play a major role in choosing the dwelling area. The workers in the diamond industry are relatively homogeneous in social character, as they generally belong to the Patidar caste from Saurashtra, north of Gujarat State. They are settled in Mahidarpura and Varachha Road in the south-eastern and eastern parts of the city. These areas are more expensive compared to the slums elsewhere. But people prefer to pay a little more and live in their own society, rather than in cheaper accommodation in alien surroundings. Comparatively, textile workers are heterogeneous in social character. They are migrants from U.P., Maharashtra, Orissa, Andhra Pradesh, Punjab, Rajasthan etc. A significant proportion has come from different regions within the state also. They form clusters of settlements wherever cheap land is available. That is why a majority of workers in the slums are textile workers (Shah 1989).

A number of large-scale industries have come up in Surat since 1984. They are generally capital-intensive industries with low output-employment ratio. They are generally situated in the outskirts of the city, forming their own campus. The employees are generally from outside the state. Employment conditions and wage-levels are much better in this sector (Shah 1994).

Besides industries, Surat experiences two major money spinning unproductive activities; speculation in land and sale of illicit liquor. The increasing flow of migrants in the city results in shortage of dwelling space. Consequently, the price of land rises leading to speculative activities in land. A strong builders' lobby is gradually emerging in the city, which experienced the highest price of land within the state, during 1981-91. Increasing construction activity in the city attracts migrant labourers from poorer areas with consequent increase in the number of slums.

The second important source of easy money is the business in illicit liquor, as Gujarat is a dry state. Drinking liquor is a socially accepted custom even in middle-class and lower middle-class families in the state. Producers, carriers and sellers maintain a good relationship with the police and the authorities for smooth functioning. A sizable number of carriers are women. Police sources reveal that there are around 500 liquor dens involving 4500 persons in the city. According to law, a person over 45 years of age can keep a certain quantity of liquor on medical grounds only. In reality however, the leakage in the system results in pumping money into individual purses at the cost of the exchequer.

TABLE 12

Major Industrial Activities and Employment in Surat: 1994

Major industries	Production (Rs. crore)	Export (Rs. crore)	Employment (lakh)
Textile	7750 (44.79)	175 (12.10)	4.50 (57.69)
Diamond	8000 (46.24)	8000 (96.38)	2.50 (32.05)
Colour chemicals	1550 (8.95)	125 (1.50)	0.80 (10.25)
Total	17300 (100.00)	8300 (100.00)	7.80 (100.00)

Source: Southern Gujarat Chamber of Commerce and Industry, Industrial Data - 1994.

Note: Figures in parentheses are percentage to corresponding total.

Diamond and textiles industries account for about an equal share in the total industrial production in the city. Diamond industry is export-based, while the other industries primarily cater to the domestic market. The textile industry accommodate more than 50 percent workers of the city, while the diamond industry provides employment to (approximately) one-third of the total work force (Table 12).

Surat's strong economic strength has created an increasing market for the vast hinterland area surrounding the city. There are two big agricultural markets in the city, supplying vegetables, milk and other agricultural products. The city in return supplies banking, educational and medical services to the hinterland. The hinterland area extends as far as 20 miles away from the city centre.

The Tertiary Sector

The tertiary sector has also experienced substantial growth during the last thirty years. Shops also grew faster during the last decade. The growth-rate was lower for offices and recreation centres during the last decade as compared to the previous one though in absolute numbers, the increase in commercial and recreational centres is over stressing the transport sector as well as the road capacity.

TABLE 13

Growth of Activities in the Tertiary Sector in Surat: 1971-91

Item	1971 (No.)	1981 (No.)	1991 (No.)	Growth rate 1971-81	Growth rate 1981-91
Shops	8915	20573	50155	8.72	9.32
Offices	10723	28586	62139	10.30	8.07
Recreation Centres	430	1031	2013	9.13	6.91

Sources: Surat Municipal Corporation; Surat Urban Development Authority.

The expanding economic activities of the city have been instrumental in the expansion of the city area in all directions specially in the south. Expansion of area, which usually creates more skewed spatial concentration and over stressed city infrastructure (Hicks 1961), however has led to many diseconomies in the city including congestion and environmental hazards. Overwhelmed by the diseconomies of size and density, the city corporation has more people and problems than it can cope with.

4. Organizational Setup for Provision and Management of Civic Amenities

In the present set-up the Surat Municipal Corporation (SMC) is the most important organizational unit responsible for the provision of basic amenities in the city. The Surat Municipality as an entity of the local self-government was established in 1853. After Independence the city's administrative boundary and structure has changed often. It became borough Municipality in 1952 and then a corporation in 1966.

The corporation is governed according to the provisions of the Bombay Provincial Municipal Corporation (BPMC) Act (1949) by a democratically elected body. The city, until very recently was divided into 36 municipal wards and 97 elected corporators used to represent the wards in the elected body. After the introduction of the Constitution (74th Amendment) Act (1992) and consequent amendment in the BPMC (1949) Act the territorial boundaries of wards have been changed. As a result while the number of wards has been lowered to 33 the number of corporators has been increased to 99, each ward now to be represented by three corporators.

According to the provisions of the BPMC (1949) Act, the SMC like any other local body consists of two municipal wings the elected or deliberative and the executive. The General Body, the Standing Committee and other special committees are under the deliberative wing. The General Body is the council of elected representatives headed by the Mayor and a Deputy Mayor who are elected by the councillors. The Standing Committee is also a body of a specified number of elected representatives who are appointed by the General Body. The Standing Committee is headed by a Chairman selected by the members of the committee. There are several special committees for different functional units. At present there are 12 such committees. The Commissioner and the other officers form the executive wing of the municipal body which is appointed by the state government. The Commissioner is the executive head of the Corporation.

Unlike other metropolitan cities where several statutory bodies have been formed encroaching upon the authority of the local self government, Surat does not have multiple authorities for providing basic amenities. Except for city transport, electricity and law and order, the city government in Surat is statutorily solely responsible for providing almost all the other services to the city dwellers. The BPMC Act specifies at least 25 matters as the obligatory duties of the corporation for which it is incumbent on the corporation to make reasonable and adequate financial and other provisions. Some of the important obligatory functions are as follows:

i) Watering, scavenging and cleaning of all public streets and places and the removal of all sweepings therefrom.
ii) Collection, removal, treatment of sewage, offensive matter and rubbish.
iii) Construction, maintenance of drains and drainage, public latrines, water closets, urinals.
iv) Lighting of public streets, municipal markets.
v) Construction or acquisition and maintenance of public hospitals.
vi) Maintaining, aiding and suitably accommodating schools for primary education.
vii) Fire brigade services.
viii) Construction and maintenance of roads and bridges.
ix) Management and maintenance of all municipal water works etc. for a sufficient supply for public and private purposes.
x) Regulation and abatement of offensive and dangerous trades and practices.
xi) Birth and death registration.
xii) The construction and maintenance of residential quarters for the municipal conservancy staff etc.

The BPMC Act (1949) also provides a list of 42 discretionary duties like provision of maternity and infant welfare homes, swimming pools, dairies, public parks, gardens and so on.

The corporation performs the above functions through various functional departments like Housing, Drainage and Public Works Water Supply, Health and Hospitals, Town Planning, Accounts etc. These are managed by senior officials such as Director of Planning, City Engineer, Additional City Engineer, Medical Officer, three Deputy Commissioners and three Assistant Commissioners. There are several smaller units under each department.

The city has very recently been divided into six zones headed by six senior officers for decentralized administration. The SMC already had 36 ward offices which now have come under the zonal offices.

Besides SMC, the other agencies which are involved in the provision of services are the Surat Electricity Company (SEC), Gujarat State Electricity Board (GSEB), Gujarat State Road Transport Corporation (GSRTC) and Surat Urban Development Authority (SUDA). The SEC is responsible for providing electricity to domestic and industrial consumers within the city limit, though the newly acquired areas in the city are still served by GSEB. The GSRTC is responsible for city bus services. To look into the balanced development of the city and its adjoining areas Surat Urban Development Authority (SUDA) was formed in 1978 by the Government of Gujarat. The SUDA area covering 772 sq. km. encompasses the city and 148 villages around Surat Municipal Corporation (SMC) boundary. SUDA is responsible for formulating the Master Plan for the city and its periphery and also for regulating the planned urban development according to the Master Plan. It chalked out the first Master Plan in 1980 for the years 1980-2000.

The Municipal Corporation of Surat develops the city within the municipal boundaries through various Town Planning

Schemes. The town planning activities of the city and its peripheral areas are guided by the Gujarat Town Planning and Urban Development Act (1976). The development activities within the city limits were earlier conducted by the Bombay Town Planning Act 1954. Among other similar Acts which have important bearings on city development is the Urban Land (Ceiling and Regulation) Act (ULCRA) enacted by the Central Government in 1976. The ULCRA was enacted with a vision to have a systematic and planned development of the urban areas and make land available to all sections of the people.

CHAPTER III

The City and its Problems

DESPITE the fact that the remarkable growth in the industrial and economic activities in the city and its periphery has made Surat a centre of wealth and resources, the quality of human life has not changed for the better. In fact it has created a densely populated core city area with congestion and deteriorating physical amenities. The city government could not cope with the excessive population growth owing to the sudden influx of migrant labourers who came from different parts of the country to get employment in ever expanding industrial activities. Also, the frequent expansions in the area on political and economic grounds without any provision for physical and social infrastructure created enormous problems for the city in terms of access to basic amenities and quality of life. The city at present suffers from deficiencies in almost all fronts of healthy development.

1. Problems Related to Urban Planning

i) The SUDA was formed in 1978 with the mandate to control unplanned development in the peripheral areas of Surat. The first Master Plan of SUDA was formulated in 1980 for the period of 1980 to 2000. The Plan had the laudable objective to achieve restructuring the city, by means of conservation, redevelopment or new development and to serve as a long term perspective to guide future developments with the broad principles: a) achievement of better environmental living conditions for the masses in a most economic way, and b) location of new population and employment centres where there is greater possibility of choice of transport route and mode available (SUDA 1980).

These objectives however were hardly fulfilled. Development did not take place according to the Master Plan in peripheral areas. Apart from unprecedented industrial development and consequent population growth several other factors are responsible for this.

Usually the "Master Plans of big cities focus only on the physical aspects of city development imposing segregation of activities like residential, industrial etc. They completely neglect the implementation process that is resource allocation, costs, phases, participants, public and private investments and more seriously the socio-economic processes taking place in the city" (Hoshino 1994). The Master Plan of SUDA is no exception. Moreover unlike other development authorities in the country, namely the Delhi Development Authority, the Calcutta Metropolitan Regional Development Authority etc., the SUDA does not possess sufficient financial resources or mandate to undertake development activities according to the Master Plan within its jurisdiction so that it can regulate and coordinate meaningfully the integrated development of the region. As a result in the absence of proper infrastructure development in the surrounding areas the city services faced tremendous pressure. This led to irregular development, substandard and illegal houses, massive encroachment of land by both rich and poor in the city and tremendous shortage in basic amenities. The poor usually have settled in flood prone, polluted, topographically difficult areas where service delivery is extremely inadequate. The results of all this have been a general deterioration of the environment and quality of life.

ii) Mixed land use pattern has led to extreme congestion in the core city area. The walled city area is the core of the city and the main centre having all types of commercial activities. It has all the market establishments, hotels and restaurants. All the cinema houses of the city are also concentrated in the core of the city. The walled city of Surat in general depicts a highly congested and high density pattern of development. There is heavy concentration of small scale and household industries especially the handlooms, small diamond cutting units and zari industries in the inner city area. The wholesale and retail trade in foodgrains and pulses, poultry and fish, vegetable and fruits, yarn and garments and a variety of shops and establishments on the one hand and burgeoning powerlooms and the diamond industry on the other continue to exist in the thickly populated areas in the walled city (CRRI 1989).

The city does not have any residential area free of mixed land use. All the residential areas have a fair amount of industrial and commercial establishments. Defining diamond and powerloom industries as cottage industries has led to their enormous growth in the residential areas. The city at present has four lakh powerlooms spread over 30000 units. There are about 250 to 260 process houses and nearly 400 texturisers. In addition there are zari industries mostly located in dingy by-lanes in the city which produce almost 80 percent of the total zari output of the country. The work conditions in most of these units are unhygienic with 10 to 15 artisans crowded together in small rooms replete with machines and highly toxic chemicals like potassium cyanide which are serious health hazards.

iii) The growing population of the city has not been evenly distributed over the extended areas. The 8.18 sq. km. area of the walled city and 47.37 sq. km. of inner periphery together constituted 71 percent of total population of the city in 1991. The outer periphery of 55.60 sq. km. which was included in the corporation boundary in 1986 constituted only 29 percent of the total population. As a result, as it has been noted before, the tiny walled city area has a population density of 51,876 persons, the inner periphery has 13,598 persons living in one sq. km. area, while the outer periphery area has only 7,739 persons per sq. km.

iv) The floor space Index (FSI) in the walled city which is higher than even in Bombay and Ahmedabad has further contributed to the congestion of the area.

v) According to various sources the restrictive clauses of the ULCRA and innumerable bye-laws resulted in massive violation of laws by unscrupulous means. The builders' lobby has become all influential. Many unauthorized buildings have been constructed, violating laws of town planning which not only increase congestion in the city but also cause further deterioration in sanitation (Shah 1994). Traffic jams, poor drainage, water shortage, air pollution, uncleaned garbage are the symptoms of deteriorating living conditions in the city.

The big builders seem to have done as they pleased. Till recently violations indulged in by builders were overlooked. But as the city problems are mounting, the public spotlight is much harsher. Both politicians and officials complain about the massive violation of building bye-laws by the builders.

The theory often put forward by the municipal officials is that two building plans are prepared by the builders. One is submitted to the corporation authorities for approval and the other is followed during the actual construction. There is a vast difference between what is approved and what is constructed. Violations are often made after a completion certificate is obtained from the authorities. After the construction is made it is not easy to demolish the structure. The stay orders from courts often restrain the authorities to take any step in this regard. Interference by interested political parties in protecting the builders has also been highlighted by the officials.

2. Housing Needs

The recent spurt in construction activities however has not been enough to solve the housing problems of the city. The massive growth of population and lack of balanced development in all the extended areas through infrastructure provision has created enormous housing problems in the city. The new industrial complexes grown within and outside the surrounding areas like Hajira, Sachin and GIDC complexes, Pandesara, Katargam etc. have created excessive pressure on the limited housing and basic infrastructural facilities. Most of the industries do not provide residential facilities to their employees. Though reliable data on housing stock are not available for the city, the trend shows that the increase in housing stock has been limited and it could not keep pace with the increasing demand. Even with high FSI and extensive vertical growth, there has been a significant gap between the number of households and the total housing stock in the old city area.

The curious feature of the housing scenario in Surat is important to note. Table 14 shows that during 1971-81, the growth in residential housing stock was much below the growth in the number of households. While the number of households grew by 21.34 percent, the housing stock for residential purposes increased by 18.19 percent. The decade of the eighties however observed a reverse trend. The number of households practically declined in the inner city area by 3.84 percent but the housing stock increased by 3.37 percent. As a net result between 1971 and 1991 the growth of housing stock has exceeded the growth in the number of households. The housing stock increased by 22.18 percent, while the number of households increased by 16.67 percent. Even then however the increased housing stock could not cope with the backlog. Although the housing shortage which was 25.06 percent in 1971, shot up to 27.02 percent in 1981 and came down to 21.54 percent in 1991, the housing needs of more than one fifth of the total households remained unfulfilled. The Surat Urban Development Authority estimated in 1980 that there was a backlog of about 60,000 dwelling units all over the city in 1971. According to its estimate, addition to new housing stock was only about 1500 to 2000 per year, while the demand for new housing stock was 10,000 per year. Although the construction activity has accelerated at a tremendous pace since SUDA made its last estimates, it has not solved the housing problems of

TABLE 14

Growth in Number of Households and Housing Stock in Old City of Surat in Eighties and Nineties

	Total housing stock			Percentage change		Total change (per cent)
	1971	1981	1991	1971-81	1981-91	1971-91
No. of households	72741	88265	84871	21.34	-3.84	16.67
No.of occupied Residential houses	54501	64415	66588	18.19	3.37	22.18
Shortage in housing stock	18230 (25.06)	23850 (27.02)	18283 (21.50)	-	-	-

Source: Compiled from Tables 2.5 and 2.9 in Das, 1994.

Note: Figures in parentheses depict the housing shortage in percentage.

the city. The recent corporation estimates show that in 1991 number of houses in the SMC area was 4,32,917 when the number of households were 2,99,389. But as a significant number of constructed houses remain vacant (83,847) and a large number of houses are used for industrial purposes (66,012), the number of residential houses (2,83,058) falls much short of the number of households. Therefore houses are being constructed in the periphery but are not being occupied because of absence of basic facilities like roads, water, electricity etc. As a result each house consists of more than one family which further aggravates the congestion in the core city area.

3. Slums and Squatter Settlements

The city projects a curious scenario so far as human settlement is concerned. On one side the city skyline is dotted with numerous high rise buildings in prime localities, on the other topographically vulnerable areas like river banks, both sides along the railway tracks and the low lying areas have been taken over by the mushroom growth of slums and unauthorized colonies of poor migrant households.

The share of slum population to the total city population which was 19.63 percent in 1973 had increased to 27.5 percent in 1992 (Das 1994). During the last one decade, that is between 1982 and 1992, the growth has been the maximum. In absolute numbers the slum population has grown from 93,000 in 1973 to 4.33 lakhs in 1992. The number of slums also increased from 145 in 1973 to nearly 300 in 1992.

Table 15 shows the trends in the growth in slum population in major cities of Gujarat during the last two decades. The table shows the slum population in major cities at three points of time. While figures for 1973 and 1981 are actual slum population estimated by different agencies, the figures for 1990 are the projections of the Town and Country Planning Organisation (TCPO), based on the previous trends. The table shows that during 1973-81 Surat experienced much faster growth in slum

TABLE 15

Slum Population in Major Cities of Gujarat

City	1973		1981		1990		Growth in slum population	
	No. (in lakhs)	% to total population	No. (in lakhs)	% to total population	No. (in lakhs)	% to total population	1973-81 (%)	1981-90 (%)
Ahmedabad	2.72	17.11	5.36	20.3	11.33	39.38	97.06	111.38
Bhavnagar	0.23	10.39	0.46	14.9	0.81	21.48	100.00	89.13
Jamnagar	0.45	20.78	0.78	24.6	0.91	26.00	73.33	16.66
Rajkot	0.21	6.85	0.79	17.8	1.35	22.05	276.19	70.89
Surat	0.93	19.63	2.32	25.4	3.39	22.61	149.46	46.12
Vadodara	0.49	10.67	1.18	15.8	2.42	23.45	140.82	105.08

Sources: Government of Gujarat (1991) for 1973 figures; Town and Country Planning Organisation (1985) for 1981 actual and 1990 projected figures.

population than all the other cities in Gujarat except Rajkot. Surprisingly, however, during 1981-90 Surat's slum population was perceived to grow at a much slower pace by only 46.12 percent which was lower than the growth rates of all the other cities except Jamnagar. However in reality the actual slum population grew much faster and crossed the 4 lakh mark according to the recent estimates. Now Surat stands next to Ahmedabad in terms of total slum population.

The slums in Surat are primarily situated on encroached municipal land, but slums on private land also constitute a significant proportion. Table 16 shows the status of ownership of land in the slums of Surat. The proportion of households living on government and municipal land together has increased from 46.9 percent to 54.3 percent during the last 20 years.

Usually the slums on privately owned land are concentrated in the peripheral areas of the city. The slums in the inner city areas are located primarily on government and municipal land. This suggests that the peripheral areas which belonged to private land owners were brought gradually within the city limits and the poor localities within the extended city limits were declared as slums because of scant and inadequate basic amenities.

TABLE 16

Status of Land Occupied by Slum Households in Surat

(*in percentage*)

Ownership of land	1973	1992
Private	43.7	37.3
Government	4.7	13.3
Municipality	42.2	41.0
Others	9.4	8.4

Sources: Surat Urban Development Authority, 1981; Das, 1994.

A recent study by Biswaroop Das (1994) shows that a maximum number of slums or about 70 percent of them are located in the eastern and south-eastern part of the city and the slums in the southern part, where the activities related to industry are concentrated, though smaller in number contain a maximum number of slum households.

The slums are primarily inhabited by migrant population. About 80 percent of all the slum households in the city are migrants from rural areas of Surat district, other districts of Gujarat and also from other states of the country. The households live in extremely unhygienic conditions. As high as 86 percent of the dwelling units are one-room tenements and 58 percent of them are not more than 100 to 200 sq. ft. in area.

Extensive survey of the slum areas by our research team also confirmed the observation. The pressure on space is such that as in Bombay slums, sometimes one small rented room is shared by 10 to 12 migrant labourers on a shift basis. Most of the units are kachcha. Even so the owners sometimes obtain high rents from the tenants. Rents vary from place to place depending on the location of the slums. Those parts of the city which house a larger number of industry related slums contain a larger proportion of rent paying households than in the other parts.

As the economic opportunities in Surat are still better than their own home states or the rural areas of Gujarat where they come from, these migrant labourers somehow get absorbed in the city workforce and earn reasonably well. But it becomes really very difficult for them to meet the high cost of living in the city after sending money for the family back home.

Access to basic amenities is minimal for these slum dwellers. Though the slums in old city area are connected by piped water supply and some of the slums even have individual water connections, the slums in the extended area are not yet covered by a water supply network. Though handpumps have been provided in these areas, because of industrial effluents seeping into the ground, water from these handpumps is often contaminated and not fit for drinking. The corporation tries to provide drinking water through water tankers but the supply is extremely limited. Most of the slum dwellers we talked to during our survey identified water supply as the most critical problem and urgently felt need of the locality.

TABLE 17

Basic Amenities in Slums of Surat

	Amenity	1973	1992
1.	Private water taps (% household)	7.00	18.9
2.	Private latrine (% household)	2.00	20.93
3.	Separate electricity connection (% household)	7.79	25.01
4.	Private ownership of land (% household)	33.32	37.30
5.	Drainage facility (% slums)	16.00	40.00
6.	Private water connection (in slums (No.)	2062	23040
7.	Public stand posts (No.)	343	1299
8.	Households per public stand post (No.)	45	72
9.	Persons per stand post (No.)	236	334
10.	Private latrines (No.)	550	19667
11.	Public toilets (No.)	655	558
12.	Households per public toilet (No.)	23	168
13.	Person per public toilet (No.)	377	777

Sources: Surat Urban Development Authority, 1980; Shah, 1989; Das 1994.

The slum surveys conducted by different agencies at different points of time confirm that access to services has improved to a certain extent during the last two decades, nevertheless a large section of slum households are still deprived of minimum basic amenities. Table 17 shows the availability of selected facilities in slums in 1974 and 1992 as obtained from different surveys. The table shows that the number of private toilets and private water connections has increased manifold during the last two decades. But the population pressure has increased much more. The facilities are still far from adequate. The number of households and persons served by one public water post or public toilet is much more today than what it was twenty years back.

Lack of basic amenities coupled with inadequate health facilities creates serious health problems in the slum areas. The corporation health centres are either far away or do not stock proper medicines. The slum dwellers have to depend on private doctors or go to quacks. Because of unhealthy surroundings the incidence of diseases like Malaria, Tuberculosis, different types of fever and water-borne diseases is high among the slum dwellers.

Slum Improvement Initiatives of the SMC

Providing basic amenities to nearly 28 percent of the total population staying in over 300 slums located in different parts of the city is one of the major challenges the SMC is facing today. Therefore, considering the specific socio-economic circumstances in which the people live in these localities, the SMC has to evolve a strategy which is able to improve the living conditions of the slum dwellers by efficient delivery of civic amenities. Although in the administrative setup of the SMC there is no department specific to slums, the problems of the slum dwellers are being handled through a host of other measures. In this manner almost all the departments of the SMC relating to health, housing and civic amenities of the slums are involved to some extent in slum development.

Besides, various special committees have been constituted by the corporation from time to time to look after various functions and activities of the SMC as directed by the state government. The list of such committees has been given in the following chart.

CHART 1
Policy Making Committees of the SMC

1. Health Committee
2. Public Works Committee
3. Water Works Committee
4. Town Planning and Town Development Committee
5. Social Welfare, Recreation and Cultural Committee
6. Drainage Committee
7. Law Committee
8. Hospital Committee
9. Housing and Garden Committee
10. Slum Improvement Committee
11. Light and Fire (Extinguishing) Committee
12. Gas Committee

It is clear from the preceding chart that there is a slum improvement committee of the SMC to monitor its measures pertaining to slum improvement and to suggest steps for the welfare of the slum dwellers.

The SMC in addition to its own efforts for providing basic amenities is also administering a few centrally sponsored programmes for the upliftment of the poor and the slum dwellers aiming at the welfare of the urban poor. These programmes are Integrated Child Development Scheme (ICDS), Urban Community Development (UCD), Urban Basic Services for the Poor (UBSP) and Nehru Rozgar Yojana (NRY). However, only UBSP is associated to some extent with the delivery of civic amenities since NRY is essentially an income generating programme for the poor, while the ICDS provides basic health and pre-nursery education to the children and UCD primarily runs vocational training schemes for the slum dwellers and provides family health advice. The social welfare, recreation and cultural committee of the SMC proposes all policy decisions pertaining to the UCD and the UBSP programmes to the standing committee of the corporation for an appropriate decision at their level and then these are approved for implementation.

The UCD which was launched in the city in 1967 with the objective of strengthening the people's participation in the city's affairs could achieve limited success only. Since its inception the UCD has covered only 1,90,017 persons belonging to 33,562 families of economically, socially and educationally backward classes in three phases (Table 18). This is less than even half of the total population living in slums at present.

TABLE 18

Progress of UCD Programme in Surat

Project	Year of inception	Covered families	Population
First	1967	10,368	61,861
Second	1978	12,376	70,105
Third	1985	10,818	58,051

Source: UCD/UBSP Office, SMC, 1994.

The UBSP is comparatively a new programme launched in 1990 which aims at giving proper attention to women and children and helps them raise their living standards. Besides providing health, nutrition and non-formal education to children and adults it has a specific goal to help provide clean potable water and waste disposal in a hygienic way.

Compared to UCD the coverage of UBSP is extremely limited. It has been able to cover only 14,400 households with a total population of 62,000 till now (Table 19) and the impact of the programme is not so visible so far as basic amenities are concerned.

The field visit by the research team of this study to some of the slums in the city has indicated that the overall impact of these programmes in keeping them clean and motivating the people to live in hygienic conditions in these areas has been extremely limited. This is partly because of the programmes' greater emphasis on different social and economic activities and partly because of fund constraints. Obviously, there is a growing need to emphasise the significance of these relatively neglected aspects of urban living in the implementation of these programmes. Particular thrust should be given on road and lane maintenance, storm water drainage, improved toilet facilities and a better garbage disposal system in the slums of Surat.

TABLE 19

Progress of UBSP Programme in Surat

Year	Households	Population	Amount (*in lakhs*)
1990-91	1000	5000	8.00
1991-92	3000	15000	8.00
1992-93	6000	20,000	5.00
1993-94	4400	22000	8.00

Source: UCD/UBSP Office, SMC, 1994.

Besides the above, the SMC also undertook some programmes for slum development on its own in the eighties with World Bank assistance. The impact of all these programmes however was negligible.

The allocation of funds for slum improvement from SMC's own sources was also too meagre to tackle the massive problem although SMC is obliged to spend at least 10 percent of its budgetary allocation for slum improvement.

Table 20 shows the expenditure on slum improvement by SMC in different years during the last decade. It is observed that the expenditure hovered only around 2 to 4.5 percent of the total expenditure of the SMC.

TABLE 20
Expenditure on Slum Improvement in Surat

(*Rs. in '000*)

Total	1980-81	1982-83	1984-85	1986-87
Total expenditure (Revenue + Capital)	152505	229024	340879	601119
Expenditure on slum improvement	3990	10477	6944	13731
(% to total expenditure)	(2.62)	(4.57)	(2.04)	(2.28)

Source: Datta, 1990.

4. Basic Amenities in the City

Industrial development in Surat accompanied by rapid population increase has led to severe pressure on the city's infrastructure. There is a growing mismatch between the demand and supply of civic amenities which is contributing to the frequent occurrences of various diseases and epidemics. Even in the wake of the city's haphazard growth the authorities are concentrating on the short term perspective of the delivery of civic amenities without taking into account the changing behaviour of the people and their requirements on planned and long term basis. Not surprising, therefore, these are the serious shortcomings in the delivery of civic amenities. The following sections highlight this phenomenon.

Water Supply Facilities

Surat boasts of having one of the oldest water works in the country. The water works were constructed as far back as in 1895. Now the supply of potable water is one of the most important obligatory duties of the corporation. The Water

Supply Department along with the Hydraulic Department in the corporation manages the water supply system in the city.

The main source of water for the city is the river Tapi. In addition there are several borewells in different parts of the city provided by the corporation and also installed by individuals. The city water supply network through its two major water works at Varachha and Sarthana produces 200 million litres of water per day. However this is only 50 percent of the installed capacity of the two water works. The corporation water network covers 70 percent of its total population and only 50 percent of its total area through its 4 distribution centres located at different parts of the city. It has 1,06,000 water connections and nearly 95 percent of them are in the domestic category. The SMC has not adopted a universal metering system. Of all the water connections only 3,568 are metered. Although Surat is a city with a high concentration of industries, the number of water consuming industries is not many within the city area. Therefore, industrial consumption does not put much pressure on the city water supply system. It is estimated that non-domestic demand is only 20 percent of the total quantity of water supplied by the SMC. Despite this, the domestic demand is not fulfilled.

Most of the extended area which was added to the city in 1986 is not yet covered by the corporation water supply. In these areas drinking water is supplied by corporation tankers. The SMC also operates 50 borewells is these areas. Water from these borewells is supplied through public stand posts. Usually supplied once a day in phases in different zones the supply of water is extremely limited in quantity. Municipal authorities confirmed that no area gets water supply for more than two hours a day. The supply starts early in the morning in phases and reaches some of the areas after 10 O'clock at night. People have to get up early in the morning or keep awake till late at night for collecting and storing their day's supply. As against the average domestic demand of 135 litres per capita per day (lpcd) the supply usually is 90 lpcd, though it varies across different zones. The supply is as low as 32 lpcd in the west zone.

As Surat is very near the sea and has a long coast line, the ground water is saline. Borewells do not provide a reliable source of drinking water. The construction of a dam at Ukai upstream of the river Tapi, has reduced the recurrence of floods in the city, but it has also deprived the city to a certain extent of its main source of water.

Even though the quantity of water supplied by the SMC per day has increased from 15 million gallons (mgd) in 1960 to 20 mgd in 1970, 35 mgd in 1980 and since then it has doubled to 70 mgd in 1989, it is far short of the total water needs of the city.

Several factors are responsible for the acute water shortage in the city:

i) *Increase in demand*: The city population grew faster than what was projected. During the last decade while population grew 66 by percent, daily water supply grew by only 33.77 percent during 1980-81 to 1991-92. (Table 21). Owing to economic prosperity and change in life style various water consuming fixtures have also been common in modern residential buildings. Both these factors have contributed to excessive demand for water in the domestic category.

ii) *Decline in raw water yield*: After the commissioning of the Ukai reservoir in 1974, the chances of washing out the deposited silt declined in the absence of flushing floods in the river during the monsoon. The excess silt deposition reduced the flow of water to infiltration wells and thus lowered the raw water yield.

iii) *Excess leakage*: The leakage in the distribution system is also quite high in Surat. As against 10 percent average leakage in a distribution system it is around 25 percent in the city. Even after the creation of a Special Leak Detection and Prevention Cell in the water department of the SMC the amount of leakage could not be brought down effectively. As a result though the total water generated is 200 mld, only 150 mld water is supplied through the system.

TABLE 21

Average Daily Water Supply, Income from Water Charges and O and M Expenditure in SMC

Year	Average supply of water per day (in'000 gallons)	Income from water charges and water taxes (Rs. in '000)	Expenditure towards O & M (Rs. in '000)
1980-81	30127	6121	9719
1981-82	31419	8373	11986
1982-83	29384	8613	14685
1983-84	27023	7547	15268
1984-85	29306	8648	18016
1985-86	32072	12340	20885
1987-88	39126	15537	36093
1991-92	40000	19300	50000

Sources: Shah, 1989; Annual Report, SMC, 1991-92.

iv) Resource constraint : The augmentation of the system needs increased financial flow which the corporation is unable to provide from its own sources. Income from service charges for water supply is abysmally low which is not enough even to support the maintenance expenditure. Municipal records show that operation and maintenance expenditure has always remained exceptionally high compared to the income from water charges. The gap between maintenance expenditure and income from water has gradually widened over time (Table 21). The income from water charges could not keep pace with the expenditure incurred on operation and maintenance. While the income has increased by 3.15 times during 1980-81 to 1991-92, the expenditure has gone up by 5.14 times. The officials allege that the meagre income from water supply is due to the ridiculously low water rates charged by the corporation. These rates do not have sufficient progressivity either (see Table 22). Rates are not higher for high value property owners. Moreover the rates have not been revised at all during the last seventeen years.

TABLE 22

Structure of Water and Conservancy Taxes in SMC: 1993-94

Net Rateable Value (Rs)	General Tax (Rs)	Water Tax		Conservancy Tax
		Residential	Commercial	
1 - 600	-	36 (Rs.)	60 (Rs.)	24 (Rs.)
601 - 800	12	36	60	3 (%)
801 - 1000	12	36	60	3
1001 - 2500	12	36	60	3
2501 - 3600	12	36	60	3
3601 - 4500	12	1 (%)	60	3
4501 - 5001	12	1	60	3
5001 - 6000	15	1	1 (%)	3
6001 - 7500	15	1	1	3
7501 - 10000	20	1	1	3
10001 - 20000	25	1	1	3
Above - 20000	30	1	1	3

Source: Surat Municipal Corporation, 1994.

The corporation has taken some initiatives in recent times to augment the water supply. Some new water projects are going on and it has contacted a French company also for commissioning future water treatment projects. The Tata Consulting Engineers (TCE) was commissioned for studying the water supply system of the city as a whole, project future demand, estimate cost and suggest strategies for meeting the future challenges. The TCE has done an extensive survey of the system and submitted its draft report in December 1994. After taking into consideration the factors such as increased population, leakage, per capita water demand in different types of settlements, it has estimated that the total water demand for Surat to be 490 million litres per day (mld) in 2001, 660 mld in 2011 and 820 mld in 2021. The total generated water may be around 300 mld within a few years after the on-going projects are completed. Therefore, to meet the future shortfall of 520 mld in 2021 the corporation has to construct many more water plants in the near future.

The corporation has approached the World Bank for a loan of Rs. 420 crores for an integrated project of water supply and drainage network, 75 percent of the cost is to come from the World Bank on condition that 25 percent will be the contribution of SMC from its own fund. However to meet the conditions the SMC needs to enhance its water rates manifold. Corporation officials as well as prominent citizens are skeptical whether the taxes can be enhanced at all. The experiences in a previous World Bank project in the 1980s, which had four components, namely, storm water drainage, area development, slum upgradation and solid waste management, showed that the SMC could not keep its own commitment in most of the years. Even the budgeted estimates could never be translated into actual expenditure on such projects. The actual expenditure fell far short of the estimates in all the years (Table 23).

TABLE 23

Expenditure on World Bank Projects in 1980s

(*Rs. in lakhs*)

Year	Expenditure	
	Estimated	Actual
1985-86	160	67
1986-87	152	47
1987-88	143	19

Source: Surat Municipal Corporation, 1994.

Municipal officials feel that water charges should be at least five times more than the present rates, that too only to cover the annual maintenance expenditure. To generate resources for capital projects is an impossible agenda. They anticipate that no elected body in the corporation of any political party will agree to take unpopular decisions which will jeopardise their electoral prospects.

Our interview with the former corporators confirmed the apprehensions of the officials. A majority of them agree that the tax rate should be increased but at the same time they express their inability to do so, as such decisions are sensitive to their electoral future. Quite a few of them suggest that they would not mind if the Administrator who is now in charge takes such decisions when the elected body is not functioning. Almost all of them also suggest privatisation of selected functional areas. If the private agencies enhance the rates the elected representatives will not be directly accountable to the public.

With regard to future strategies for improving the water supply in Surat it is important to mention that after the plague outbreak there is a growing realisation at the SMC about the dismal condition of water supply in Surat. Therefore, in the annual budget for the year 1995-96 there has been a higher allocation of Rs. 32 crores for augmenting water supply in the city by undertaking capital construction like setting up some distribution stations and laying pipelines in some of the areas currently not getting piped water, including those ones which came into the corporations limit in 1986. This is a significant decision if seen in the context of general criticism of the SMC for not granting money for capital projects.

Waste Disposal

Urban waste has been traditionally looked at as solid and liquid wastes. But in the Indian context owing to the prevalence of open defecation on a large scale, the problem of human waste clearly presents a case of special attention. This practice not only creates serious environmental hazards but also encourages manual scavenging which is extremely degrading to human dignity.

The disposal systems for both liquid and solid wastes are precarious in the cities of India. Surat is no exception. The sewage disposal system of the city is utterly inadequate. The system of the old city which was installed in 1956 and was designed for a projected population of 3 lakhs has been too inadequate for the present population of the area. The water supply system has been augmented in phases at different points of time but sewerage network to carry the waste water could not be extended at the similar pace.

The excess load of waste water is being diverted through storm water drains. Only a 8.26 sq. km. area of the walled city and around 2 sq. km. area of the other part of the city are covered by the sewerage network. The network at present covers only 30 percent of the population and 13 percent of the area. The rest of the city is covered either by septic tanks or cesspools which are to be cleaned through the vacuum emptier. The vast area covered by such types of waste disposal systems needs a large number of such vacuum emptiers which the local authority does not have. As a result the cesspools overflow very often and soil get contaminated with filth.

The waste water treatment facility also is extremely limited. It is estimated that the daily flow of waste water for 14 lakhs population in 1987 at the rate of 135 lpcd was 150 mld. The treatment capacity of the SMC was only for 76 mld in two plants of 25 mld and 51 mld respectively. Half of the untreated waste water is discharged into the river Tapi. Lack of funds and also non-availability of suitable land for setting up the sewage treatment plants are cited by the officials as the most important factors inhibiting the augmentation and extension of sewage treatment facilities in the city.

The inadequacy of storm water drains also creates problems. The whole city used to experience repeated inundation by flood water till the construction of the Ukai dam. After the construction of the dam though this problem has been partially solved, the low lying areas still get submerged during heavy rains. During the flood in August-September 1994, low lying areas like Ved road and Katargam were under 8 to 10 feet of water which took several days to recede. The water mark was still visible when we visited the area in December 1994.

The SMC chalked out the Master Plan for drainage network in the city in 1983 and with financial assistance from the World Bank, the state government and from its own resources executed the storm water drainage project which was completed by the end of the last decade. The extended network also was quite inadequate to solve the city's drainage problem.

Moreover, the limited storm water drainage facility is used for different other purposes. The untreated wastes containing obnoxious chemicals by the textile and dyeing industries are discharged into the natural water body either directly or through the storm water drainage system. Most of the big industrial houses also do not have waste treatment facilities. They connect the waste water pipes to storm water drains. Therefore the limited storm water drainage facility carries both sewage and illegal discharge of industrial wastes straight to the river Tapi. This not only corrodes the pipes but creates severe environmental pollution. According to the local people during the recent flood the low lying areas were submerged not by flood waters alone but also by dirty sewage and chemical wastes which gushed out of the storm drains. According to them this only created the ground for the outbreak of plague.

The Surat Municipal Corporation under the municipal statute is obliged to restrict such activities within its area which it often fails to observe. The Gujarat Pollution Control Board under the water (Prevention and Control of Pollution) Act 1974 has sufficient powers to prohibit and even penalise the people for discharging untreated effluents into the natural water body. However the implementation of the Act has not been strict enough to deter the offenders from indulging in such activities.

Piles of uncollected garbage on the streets and the overflowing waste bins are a common sight in every metropolitan centre in India, because garbage generation far exceeds garbage removal and disposal facilities. The outbreak of plague in Surat has brought to light the inadequacy of the solid waste disposal facilities provided by the city authorities in the country. Surat produces 1040 tonnes of refuse every day at the rate of 600 grams per capita per day, of which 920 tonnes are disposed of every day according to the municipal records. But unofficial estimates state that 250 tonnes of garbage of the 1250 tonnes generated everyday are left uncollected. This is despite the fact that the corporation has the maximum staff strength in the sanitation department. The most common complaint of the people is that the municipal sweepers do not come for cleaning the streets and waste bins on a regular basis. Most of the housing society complexes have to employ private sweepers who collect domestic garbage and dump it in the municipal bins where the garbage remains uncleared for days together. People complained that in Surat 50 percent of the trucks and dumpers in the SMC are out of order on any given day.

During the recent flood hundreds of cattle and other animals died in areas submerged by flood water. The local residents alleged that the incidence of plague would not have occurred if the areas had been cleaned immediately and carcasses removed. The outbreak of the plague might be an unprecedented or unexpected happening but any type of epidemic could have taken place in the city due to prevailing filthy living conditions.

The municipal official in charge of the concerned department however claimed that all garbage bins are cleaned everyday at night but bins become full again during the day. The officials complain about the non-cooperation of the public and lack of awareness about cleanliness. People dump their household waste on the street. Several eating houses alongside the roads also throw their waste materials on the road side. The market places are littered with different kinds of refuse which even if they are cleaned regularly again pile up in no time. In addition, the industries also dump their industrial wastes like coal ashes etc. outside their premises on open grounds or roads.

The sanitation unit under the public health department of the SMC is in charge of keeping the city clean through its three operating wings - Ward Sanitation, Refuse Disposal Unit and Solid Waste Control Unit. It has sufficient staff strength also to perform the activities. However the common complaint is that absenteeism among the ground staff is extremely high - nearly 40 percent of the sweepers remain absent from duty every day. It is also alleged that during the plague half of the 2500 sweepers fled the city, many of the sweepers do private jobs during duty hours and earn extra money. The officials express their helplessness in taking any action against the erring *Safai Karmacharis* because of the protection they get under the strong labour law. They also allege that no procedural action, even dismissal from service is a deterrent for them as most of them are financially quite well off and earn much more from outside work than what they get from the corporation as salary.

The sweepers however had different stories to tell. They alleged that their work load has increased tremendously because of increase in the corporation area and also owing to population growth. But the number of employees in their category has remained the same. There has been practically no recruitment during the last few years. The number of vehicles is also few. At present each sweeper has to clean 30,000 metres of roads every day which is exactly double what was recommended by the Malkani Commission in its report. It is difficult for them to work with such limitations. They complain that after the flood, the corporation employed private contractors for removing the carcasses from flood affected areas. It is these private contractors who failed to perform their duties, not the corporation's *Safai Karmacharis.*

The allegation that they fled the city during the plague was refuted by the leaders of the sweepers' union when they said that as these sweepers belonged to the city the question of leaving the city did not arise. In fact they worked for extra hours during those days as the Corporation promised them additional monetary incentives of Rs. 50/60 a day.

Roads and Traffic

The city roads especially those in the inner city area are extremely congested. Various factors contribute to this overcrowding. .

i) The mixed land use pattern of the inner city area, limited road space coupled with excessive growth in vehicles in the city and its peripheries have made the city roads extremely congested. The 8 sq. km. of area of the inner city has 14.4 percent road space while the whole city has only 4 percent of the area demarcated as roads. The narrow width of the lanes and bylanes which were constructed ages back in the walled city area are not fit for an efficient public transport system.

ii) The Gujarat State Road Transport Corporation (GSRTC) which provides the bus transport within the city and connects the city with other nearby centres in the states has very limited service within the city. Because of a limited fleet, the city bus service suffers from the problem of non-adherence to schedules leading to hardship for the public, like overcrowding, abnormal waiting etc. As a result people mostly have to depend on their own modes of transport. Possessing a vehicle is not a luxury here but a necessity. There has been an exorbitant growth in the number of vehicles especially two-wheelers during the last two decades. According to the Central Road Research

Institute (CRRI) which was commissioned by the SMC for studying the traffic pattern of the city in 1987, while the total number of vehicles in the city increased from 12,528 in 1968-69 to 1,84,175 in 1987-88 or by 13.5 times the number of two wheelers rose from 3567 to 1,37,916 that is by 38 times during this period. In 1987-88 two wheelers constituted 75 percent of all motor vehicles in the city. The limited road space could not cope with this excessive flow of traffic.

iii) Moreover the industrial growth in Hajira-Magdalla complexes have led to increased heavy vehicle traffic flow to and from the complexes through the city. This creates further problems for the already overflowing city roads.

iv) Major industrial activities in the vicinity of the SMC area have grown tremendously over time and a migrant labour force from all over the country has flocked to the city to work in these industrial establishments, who have to stay in the city and commute to the work place daily. This has also increased the traffic flow.

v) The hinterland around the SMC area which comes under the jurisdiction of SUDA has many villages. The inhabitants of these villages are also dependent on the city for their livelihood and have to commute to the city for different purposes. The SUDA Master Plan which was formulated in 1980 had the laudable objective of 'evolving poly-nucleated structure for the area as against the present mono-centre structure by developing a few growth centres with emphasis on more district centres' (SUDA 1980). However the plan has hardly come into effect. Urban fringe areas have also not been developed according to the plan. As a result people from all these surrounding areas have to come to the city often adding to the traffic flow.

vi) Narrow roads are being regularly used for parking purposes in the absence of proper vigilance. Therefore, the continuing shortcomings with regard to improved traffic control system and effective enforcement measures have compounded the problems associated with safe and smooth traffic on the one hand and the systematic storage of stationary vehicles on the other (CRRI 1989).

The CRRI in its report submitted to the SMC in 1989 strongly suggested the shifting of some wholesale markets, commercial and industrial activities from the chronically congested parts of the walled city and also emphasized the increased use of public bus transportation rather than personal modes. However this has not taken place yet. The system has deteriorated further. A ride through the central part of the city at any point of time shows extremely congested and overcrowded roads and intersections.

Health Infrastructure and Status of Public Health

Unlike many other cities where the local bodies have very little role to play in providing health infrastructure, the Surat Municipal Corporation maintains an extensive network of hospitals, health centres, maternity homes etc. in the city. The Public Health Department (PHD) of the SMC which is headed by the Deputy Commissioner (Health and Hospital), has one General Hospital, one Infectious Diseases Hospital, three Maternity Homes, 3 Maternity homes cum Health Centres, 8 Health Centres and one dispensary, which are scattered in different parts of the city. In addition there are two mobile Dispensaries and one Homeopathic dispensary. While Maternity Homes and Maternity Homes cum Health Centres have limited arrangements for in-patients, out-patients are also treated in Health Centres and dispensaries.

Besides providing curative health facilities the SMC is maintaining a Preventive Health Department which has separate wings for epidemic control, filaria and malaria control, leprosy control, vaccination etc. The Preventive Health Care Department is supposed to check epidemics through cleanliness drives, food inspection, maintaining health laboratory, cleaning markets, and abattoirs, water bodies etc.

In addition to the medical facilities provided by the city government, the state government also runs a major hospital and a few health centres in the city.

The Public Health Department is the biggest department in the corporation. Although the number of employees in the Health Department has not increased proportionately with the total staff strength of the corporation, it has grown by nearly five times during 1971-1988. The department has always consisted of more than half of the total work force of the SMC (see Table 24).

TABLE 24

Growth of Work Force in the Health Department of SMC

	Total number of Employees		Increase during 1971-88
	1971	1988	
Municipal Corporation	1817	9631	5.3 times
Public Health Department	1027 (56.52)	4816 (50.62)	4.75 times

Source: Mehta, 1989.

Note: Figures in parentheses are percentage of the public health department employees to the total number of the SMC's employees.

The total expenditure on health has also increased considerably over time in the SMC and the maximum share of corporation expenditure also goes to the Health Department. However the expenditure on health has not grown proportionately with the total municipal expenditure. In fact, the share of health expenditure to the total expenditure has undergone a gradual decline over the years. As Table 25 shows, health expenditure which was 16.31 percent of total municipal expenditure in 1980-81 has gone down to 13.89 percent in 1986-87.

The facilities provided by the government and the corporation are quite inadequate for the burgeoning city population. Moreover the infrastructure has not grown at all over time. The existing facilities also suffer from various limitations like inadequate medical and para medical personnel, irregular supply of medicines etc. A large section of the population, therefore, go to private doctors.

TABLE 25

Actual Revenue Expenditure of SMC on Health Services

(*Rs.'000*)

Expenditure	1980-81	1982-83	1984-85	1986-87
Total revenue expenditure of the corporation	130824	197226	283348	471429
Public health	7874	13062	16102	23289
Conservancy	6302	8519	15149	26178
Health and family planning	7161	9564	12667	16006
Total health expenditure	21337	31145	43915	65473
(% to total revenue expenditure)	(16.31)	(15.79)	(15.50)	(13.89)

Source: Compiled from Datta, 1994.

The limited public sector health facility has given rise to a mushroom growth of private clinics and nursing homes, many of which are of dubious nature. The officials complain that there are about 1000 private practitioners in the city but 50 percent of them are unqualified and unregistered. These doctors mainly cater to the poorer section of the population who prefer going to them for treatment than commuting to the distant health centres which most of the time run short of medicines or involve long waiting periods. Many of these so called private medical clinics are nothing but holes in a wall, manned by people who are quacks. They are very dirty, yet they are overflowing with patients (Philipose 1994).

The corporation officials allege that it is because of the negligence and inefficiency of these irresponsible doctors that the detection of plague was delayed and the casualties for the first-three days after the detection of the disease was so high. They treated plague as any other viral fever for quite a long and when it was detected properly they were the first to flee the city in panic. Not only that, they spread panic and rumours to motivate others also to leave the city. Their closed dispensaries had to bear the brunt of the public wrath.

Whatever may be the allegation however, against the private medical network which provides only curative facilities, it may not be appropriate to hold it responsible for the inadequate and inefficient health services in the city and the frequent outbreak of epidemics. In fact a majority of the private doctors are trying to fill the void which the public sector health delivery system has created over time. Problems of solid waste disposal, inadequate sewerage treatment and disposal facilities, severe air and water pollution are the results of serious neglect of preventive health facilities which are usually the responsibilities of the public sector. It is said that in Surat there is a regular cyclical order of seasonal epidemics like malaria, typhoid, jaundice, diarrhoea and conjunctivitis from summer to the monsoon to the post-monsoon period and most of these are water borne diseases.

Usually the disease pattern in the growing cities of developing countries shows a significant change from water-to-air-borne diseases as the pollutants change from water to air with growing affluence (Webster 1994). In Surat however, as in many other fast growing cities in India, the trend is not so obvious. The growing industrial development and affluence of the city instead of solving the basic sanitation problems has aggravated them. Therefore, the incidence of water borne diseases has not gone down. At the same time excessive traffic flow and big and small industries within and around the city have increased the level of air pollution manifold. As a result along with water borne diseases the city is facing the growing incidence of new diseases as well which are attributable to air pollution.

Divergent views emerged during the course of the discussion with people of different backgrounds about the pathetic public health situation in the city. Some of them expressed the view that the corporation had no infrastructure to deal with any crisis especially epidemics like the plague. A few others argued that the response in Surat was entirely consistent with the official attitudes to health and urban development policy issues followed at the national level. Public housing and public health are not municipal or state priorities at all in most of the cities in India. Knowledgeable persons echoed the statement made by Jan Breman of the Centre for Asian Studies, Amsterdam, who has done extensive research on Surat. While commenting on the plague he said 'the epidemics have to do with the retreat of the state and the absence of a public sphere. The state has given up any pretence of being an arbiter between capital and the poor' (Ramachandran 1994).

The officials in the health department of the SMC commented that the corporation will have to provide at least 200 health centres to cover the whole city with effective treatment facilities. The SMC does not have the financial capacity to do so.

According to others, however, financial constraint is not the factor which affects the implementation of the schemes for improving the sanitation and health facilities in the city. Prominent citizens, representatives from industries and the common people accused both the SMC officials and the elected representatives for diverting the funds demarcated for such projects to those which are not so urgent and sometimes not even necessary at all on several occasions. They give more importance to discretionary duties than to the obligatory ones. People complain that instead of concentrating on more urgently felt needs like water and drainage they spend more on non-priority accounts like swimming pools, indoor stadium etc. which a very senior official of SMC called an "egoboosting extravaganza". It is alleged that for an indoor games stadium a sum of Rs. 10 crores was spent in 1989 by the previous elected body when 80 percent of the city population was not covered by any drainage facility. In addition, there are allegations of mismanagement of funds, cost escalation due to non-completion of projects on time and delay in receiving the sanction for development projects which add to the precarious situation of the public health scenario in the city.

After the plague epidemic the SMC has taken some initiatives to provide better medical facilities. The 1995-96 budget of the SMC is proposing to set up six new health centres in the city, of which four will be in so called backward areas where there are more slums. This would be in addition to the upgradation of two health centres which are again in the backward slum areas so that more facilities could be made available for the prevention as well as treatment of diseases. Besides, the SMC is also setting up a proper health education unit which was not there for so long. The aim of the health education unit will be to involve NGOs in the work of imparting health education and raising the level of awareness among the people.

CHAPTER IV

Problems of Urban Governance

THE earlier chapters have shown that during the last two decades Surat not only experienced a remarkable prosperity in the industrial and economic fields but also faced a severe crisis of basic amenities and environmental decay. The reasons for such decay are many, some of which are specific to each sector like water, sanitation, traffic etc. which have been discussed earlier. However the problems of basic services and overall deterioration in the quality of life in Surat reveals the severe lacunae in urban management. This is to a great extent due to the failure on the part of the SMC. A majority of our respondents said that the situation deteriorated faster during the last few years owing to its negligence. The recent plague is the culmination of this long neglect. Several internal problems of the SMC are affecting the functioning of the corporation. There has been a complete lack of coordination between the executive and legislative wings of the SMC. Officials and councillors could not take an integrated view to cooperate on various problems marring the city. While among different departments of the corporation there is a great deal of conflict, the councillors had also been missing an appropriate understanding and vision of the civic problems of the city. Besides, frequent political interference from various quarters has put things in a further mess. These factors can be categorized as political, administrative and financial limitations, high level of corruption within the corporation, lack of coordination with other sectoral agencies etc, which have contributed to the decay of urban governance in Surat. Apart from the internal problems of the SMC, however, there are several other external factors also which according to our respondents are responsible for the city's predicaments. These are lack of support from industries, public apathy, neglect by the state and central governments to the problems of the city, and so forth.

1. Political Participation

Absence of Elected Local Body

It is widely known that "The local government is important in environmental management because (at least in principle) it is the only multipurpose and multifunctional agency located 'on the scene' of local development projects; and when it is democratically elected and accountable, it is also the only institution that has a synoptic vision of what the whole community needs" (Stren 1994). An elected body is more responsible to the electorate and the elected representatives are better aware of the problems of the people, they get faster feedback from the people and work as a catalyst between the administration and the community. They are in a better position to feel the crisis and manage it too. They can compel the administrative authorities to take immediate and appropriate action when the situation demands. However the media reports and also many of our respondents highlighted that after the recent flood, the administration took 15 days to clear the sludge and mud and remove the carcasses from the flood affected areas. This delay, according to many, created unsanitary conditions, which supposedly led to the outbreak of plague. Even after the detection of the disease there was a serious communication gap among different agencies and the district administration took several days to declare the city as plague affected. This delay according to many especially the former corporators would not have happened if the democratically elected body were there which is entrusted with sufficient powers under the BPMC Act (1949) to declare an emergency in such a situation and take necessary action for the safety of the people.

Although the city administration along with several other governmental and non-governmental organizations faced the situation on a war footing and brought the situation under control after the initial confusion and delay, by then 60 patients had already died, several inflicted by the disease and about six lakhs people deserted the city.

Unlike many of its other counterparts, the Surat Municipal Corporation however neither had a long spell of supersession by the state government nor did it function without an elected local body for long, when the records showed that as of 1989 as many as 39 of 71 municipal corporations were in a superseded state all over the country (Jha 1993). Except the two years, the elections to the local bodies have been quite regular in the whole state of Gujarat and also in Surat. But the plague broke out when there was no elected local body. The sequence of events which took place during the last two years has provided the impetus in consolidating the conviction that a democratically elected local body is essential in effective urban management. Even the Gujarat High Court did not hesitate to point out that one of the reasons for the occurrence and spreading of plague was the absence of an elected body in Surat Municipal Corporation. In the absence of an elected local body nobody can be held responsible for the lapses (Mishra 1994).

Elections to the municipal corporations in Gujarat have been postponed repeatedly on one pretext or the other since February 1992 when the term of the previous elected bodies in the state expired. The chronology of events which led to the postponements is interesting to note:

First, elections to the local bodies were due in February 1992 but were postponed on the ground that the revised electoral roles based on 1991 census figures, the prerequisite issued by the State Election Commission, were not ready.

Second, following the High Court order on an appeal by a BJP corporator against the state government decision, a new date for holding the election was decided by the end of December 1992. However, it was again postponed in the wake of post-Ayodhya violence in the cities.

Third, the decision was again challenged in the Supreme Court and following the Supreme Court intervention the new schedule was fixed as 24 January 1993. This time also the election was postponed by the state with the help of extraordinary powers assumed under the newly enacted "Temporary Postponement and Extension of Terms Act". Instead, the terms of all the local bodies were extended up to October 1993.

Fourth, reacting again to an appeal the High Court ordered that the civic polls must be held by 12 September 1993. Elections were again postponed this time as the Legislature passed the Bombay Provincial Municipal Corporation (Gujarat, Amendment) Bill in the State Assembly.

Fifth, again on further appeal to the High Court the state government committed to hold the election by August 1994. However despite the assurance given to the court, the opposition party (BJP) joined hands with the ruling party in the state (Congress) in postponing the election to January 1995. Both the parties were scared to face the electorates.

Sixth, this time the High Court came down heavily on the state and ordered completion of the entire civic and panchayat polls in the state by the end of October 1994. Then came the plague in September. The election was again deferred on this ground. This time the High Court did not hesitate to strike down the Gujarat Local Authorities (Temporary Postponement of Election) Act 1994.

However, while the elections were held as per the court directives in 54 municipalities in December 1994, the elections to the municipal corporations in the state took place only in June 1995. They were delayed on the ground of updating of electoral roles according to newly demarcated ward boundaries, reservation of seats for women, SC/ST etc. according to the guidelines provided in the recently amended BPMC Act (1949) in the light of the 74th Constitutional Amendment Act 1992 (or Nagarpalika Act).

This high handedness by the state government even after the adoption of the 74th Constitutional Amendment was protested by many corporators. Even the officials also were unhappy with the increasing state intervention. Various instructions about the electoral roles due to change in ward boundaries with the reduction in the number of wards from 36 to 33 according to the new instruction from the State Election Commission, the change in the eligibility criteria of the prospective voters etc have made the work more difficult and extremely time consuming. They are all the more unhappy that the state government has usurped the power of the municipal corporation so far as election responsibilities in urban local bodies are concerned. So much so that the District Collector has become more important than the corporation official even in the municipal elections. Previously the Municipal Commissioner was the Electorate Registration Officer (ERO) for the municipal elections. Now the District Collector will be the ERO. Moreover, barring primary teachers no other municipal staff will be engaged in conducting the elections. Both the corporators and the officials are equally dissatisfied about the state government's hesitation in devolution of power to the local level even after the Constitutional Amendment Act (1992) came into being, more so when the corporation has to do all the cumbersome work preceding the elections.

Political Instability

Although the existence of a democratically elected body in the corporation through regular elections is extremely important, that does not automatically establish that it is the only requirement for an efficient local government. There must be stability in the governance which will help in pursuing policies and programmes on a continued basis at least for a certain period of time to prove their credibility and to respect people's verdict.

Local people said that the SMC had its best period of administration under the rule of the Janata Party during 1979 to 1981. There have been frequent changes in power in the SMC during the last few years leading to uncertainty, confusion and instability in the corporation activities. Since the 1981 till 1992 when the term of the last elected body expired, the situation has changed number of times, which the following chart may show:

CHART 2

Parties in Power in SMC since 1977 to 1993

Party in Power	From	To
Janata Party	1977	January 1981
Congress I	February 1981	June 1983
BJP	July 1983	September 1983
Congress	November 1983	February 1984
BJP	February 1984	December 1984
Congress	April 1985	February 1987
Congress	February 1987	January 1988
BJP	February 1988	June 1988
Congress I	August 1988	February 1990
BJP	February 1990	October 1993

In fact the corporation had hardly any occasion to be governed consistently by a single party for more than two years, except from 1990 to 1993 when BJP was in power. So much so that since 1987 when the last election was held till the beginning of 1990 the change of power in the SMC between BJP and Congress was almost a half yearly affair. Lack of stability arising out of constant infighting between the ruling party and the opposition and self-interest of a few elected representatives who changed their allegiance from one party to another to tilt the balance of power seriously hampered the functioning of the local body during this period.

The recent plague is the culmination of the long neglect of people's demand for reasonable basic amenities by the SMC. The elected representatives are no less responsible for this. The common people now have little faith in their political leaders. They alleged that barring a few most of the elected representatives come to visit them only before the elections. Even during last year's flood very few ex-corporators visited their constituencies for rescue operations and during the plague it was alleged that some of them even fled the city.

2. Administrative Problems

Bureaucracy vs Elected Representatives

Surat Municipal Corporation like any other urban local body in India suffers from inherent administrative deficiencies. As the National Commission on Urbanisation notes, where there are elected corporations there is very often friction between the councillors and the officials (NCU 1988). Even at the level of technical matters there is constant intervention by elected representatives. They are unable to overview the city problems as a whole and try to project the immediate needs of their individual wards.

The corporators on the other hand argue that they do not have sufficient powers under the BPMC Act (1949) according to which the SMC functions. The Act, like similar Acts for other corporations in the country, is based on separation of executive powers and functions which provides sufficient ground for conflict between the bureaucracy and the elected leaders. The Commissioner is one of the three constituents of the corporation. Though the executive powers vests in the corporation, and its executive committee, the executive functions are performed by the Municipal Commissioner appointed by the state government. The corporators express their unhappiness with the existing system. They complain that even if any resolution is passed by the elected wing it is not binding on the executive head, and they do not have sufficient power either to take action against the erring officials. If they are not happy with the Commissioner they need five-eighths voting in favour of the decision, for the removal of the Commissioner.

There is serious lack of coordination between three constituents of the local body as envisaged in Section IV of the BPMC Act (1965). There is a conflict between the statutory authorities, standing committees and special committees. There is also a conflict between executive departments. If a decision is taken by the General Body, the executive wing takes a long time to implement that. One ex-corporator complained that in July 1991 it was resolved by the General body that Town Planning Scheme of Ved road - Katargam area should be taken up on priority basis. But it was only in January 1995, after a gap of four years when the same area was affected by flood and subsequent plague, the first effort was made to formulate the Town Planning Scheme.

The corporators who are aware of the provisions of the 74th Constitutional Amendment Act 1992 and consequent amendment in the BPMC Act state that the BPMC (Gujarat Amendment) Act 1993 will not bring any significant change in the existing administrative system. They allege that the substantive executive power in the hands of a state appointed executive leads to excessive bureaucratic control and erosion in the ethos of self-governance. Both the officials and the corporators agree at one point that except for reservation of one-third seats for women and constitution of the State Finance Commission nothing much has been incorporated in the amended BPMC Act.

The functional domains of the executive and the elected representatives have remained the same. Some of the corporators even suggested that only the system of Mayor-in-Council which has been functioning in Calcutta and Howrah Corporations where the Mayor is the executive head and the Commissioner is the secretary to the Mayor-in-Council, can make the elected representatives more powerful and more accountable to the people.

Centralised Administrative System

Until very recently the decision making process in the SMC was totally centralised in the main office. The absence of a decentralised administrative system hampered the day-to-day functioning of the corporation. The corporation has 36 ward offices situated in each municipal ward but apart from day-to-day maintenance and sanitation work they do not have many functions. Since April 1994 a decentralised administrative system has been introduced in the SMC. The city now is divided into six administrative zones, each zone having a zonal office headed by a senior official of the corporation under the overall supervision of the Commissioner. The zonal offices are responsible not only for sanitation and engineering works but also for collecting revenues in the respective zones. Officials claim that this system will help them in having closer contact with the people, reduce delay in programme implementation and take immediate action when needed. Common people are however quite apprehensive about the effectiveness of the decentralised system. The people in the flood affected areas complained that the zonal office in their region did not take immediate steps to clean the garbage and dead carcasses and it was because of this negligence only that the plague broke out in those areas.

The administrative decentralisation, however has nothing to do with the opinion in decentralised decision making at the local level as envisaged under the 74th Constitutional Amendment Act. Under the Act in the case of metropolitan cities, Ward Committees are to be constituted at the ward level as the second tier of democratic decentralised system. This has been ensured in the amended BPMC Act as well. The ward committees are to consist of elected members and also a specified number of other members nominated by the state government from the local people. People are however skeptical whether formation of such committees at the ward level will in any way usher in the decentralised decision making system. They are of the opinion that according to the provision of the Act, barring the elected representatives from the respective wards, since all other members in a ward committee are nominated by the state, the autonomy of the local government will be hamperal. The state government can always implant their own candidates who may not work in tandem with the elected representatives or may not have even popular support. This may create further tension at the ground level.

Interdepartmental Coordination

Lack of interdepartmental coordination within the SMC is one of the many factors affecting the smooth functioning in the corporation. The engineering department is always in conflict with the health department. Even within a department there is often conflict between different officials and subordinate staff. Each department is following its own sectoral development plan without considering the impact on other sectors. For example, the water supply network is augmented without sufficient provision of a drainage system, municipal boundaries are extended without considering the technical and financial implications for extending services to these areas, massive construction activities are permitted in such areas where water and sewerage network are non-existent. This sectoral approach is very much detrimental to an integrated development of the city.

Coordination with other Sectoral Agencies

Although the management of urban development in the country is entrusted to local bodies, paradoxically there has been a gradual encroachment on their authorities by a number of government and semi-government special purpose bodies such as development authorities, housing boards, slum clearance boards, water and sewerage boards and so forth. The National Commission on Urbanisation observed that mushrooming of these organisations has resulted in a dichotomy in urban management in which the maintenance of the decaying and largely inadequate service becomes the responsibility of municipalities, whereas almost the entire capital input to the city expansion, together with the profits therefrom, fall to the share of the functional organisations or development authorities (NCU 1988).

Even after the recent amendment in the BPMC Act (1949) in Gujarat the functional responsibilities continues to be what it was in the past, the state intervention through parastatal organisations and specific purpose authorities still thrive in the state and the traditional municipal functions are as fragmented as before (Jha 1993).

Although the encroachment on functional domain is not so serious in the case of SMC, it has to interact always with various private agencies, parastatal authorities and regional and district offices of the state government departments, which are connected with the provision of basic services in the city. There are private agencies like Surat Electricity Corporation which provide electricity to the city, parastatal authorities like the State Urban Development Authority, Slum Clearance Board, Gujarat Municipal Finance Board etc., and the State Government agencies like Gujarat State Road Transport Corporation, Gujarat State Pollution Control Board, Police Department, the District Collector's Office and so on.

Officials complain that coordination with other sectoral agencies sometimes is a long and arduous process which leads to delay in project implementation resulting in cost and time overruns. Moreover, the state government and other agencies often take major decisions which have a direct bearing on the municipal functioning without even consulting the municipal body. The extensive industrial licensing policy of the state in the surrounding areas of Surat has affected the inner city environment which the city government has to manage. Repeated extension of the city limits without making any provision for basic amenities is also an example of utter disregard towards the principle of local autonomy.

3. Finances of Surat Municipal Corporation

The municipal bodies in the country have two sources of revenue, namely, external and internal. The major external sources are grants, shared taxes and loans. The transfer of resources from the state to the local bodies is by way of grant and shared taxes. The local bodies generally get two types of grants – general category grants and specific grants. The former covers a major portion of salary disbursement as well as deficit in the revenue account. The latter covers grants for specific projects like sanitation, roads, education, disaster relief, family planning etc. Besides these, there are capital grants, which generally decline with increases in the size of the local body. Another source of external finance is by way of loans. There are generally two kinds of loans, (a) institutional borrowing (LIC, HUDCO, World Bank etc.) and (b) open-market borrowing with government guarantee.

Tax-revenue and non-tax-revenue are two major sources of internal finance.

In Gujarat, however, the state government does not share taxes with the corporation. Except a nominal grant for education, the SMC does not receive any grant. Most of the revenue it earns is from its own sources.

Financially, the SMC is one of the most solvent corporations in the country. In the last two decades, it has experienced approximately 190 per cent increase in per-capita revenue income and more than 400 per cent increase in per-capita capital revenue. Revenue income has grown rapidly, specially in recent years, causing considerable transfer of surplus to the capital account. In Gujarat, of all the six corporations SMC has the highest per-capita total income which was on an average Rs. 771 during 1990-91 to 1992-93. Whereas for major corporations like Ahmedabad and Vadodara it was Rs. 593 and Rs. 669 respectively (Table 26).

In Gujarat usually maximum share of total revenue of any urban local body comes from its own sources, both tax and non-tax. In the case of Surat as high as 96.42 percent of its total revenue came from its own sources during 1990-93 as Table 26 shows.

TABLE 26

Per-capita Total Income and Revenue from Own Sources in Six Corporations in Gujarat: 1990-93

Corporation	Percapita total revenue (Rs.)	Percapita revenue from own sources (Rs.)	% of Revenue from own sources to total revenue.
Ahmedabad	593.46	509.12	85.72
Bhavnagar	354.23	303.77	85.09
Jamnagar	441.34	368.17	83.50
Rajkot	526.69	418.08	91.14
Surat	771.24	743.67	96.42
Vadodara	668.95	583.94	87.32

Source: Complied from National Institute of Public Finance and Policy, 1994, New Delhi.

TABLE 27

Per-capita Revenue and Expenditure of the SMC during 1971-91

(*in Rs.*)

Item	1971	1981	1991
Capital expenditure	36.89	64.64	261.20
Revenue expenditure	222.19	330.16	643.86
Capital income	31.59	58.71	160.41
Revenue income	220.71	360.03	673.07

Source: Compiled from SMC budgets.

Per capita revenue expenditure has always remained very high. Although per capita capital expenditure has always been higher than capital revenue in this account (Table 27), the expenditure has been very low till 1981. In 1991 there has been a significant rise in both capital revenue and capital expenditure. There has been visible change in the major components of revenue income during the last two decades as well. The major source of revenue has been income from octroi.

The city has benefited from increasing industrial activities, specially since the eighties. It has contributed to the municipal revenue by way of increasing the share for octroi. More than half of municipal revenue comes from octroi. Octroi revenue has increased from 59.98 percent in 1971-81 to 67.28 percent in 1981-91. The proportion of grant which was only 12.72 percent during 1971-81 has further come down to 7.69 percent during 1981-91. A perusal of the SMC budget for last few years shows that there has always been a surplus in the revenue account which is transferred to the capital account each year. The corporation is thus able to spare a substantial amount from its own sources for capital projects although it may not be sufficient to provide all the capital required to cover the whole city with minimum basic amenities. The corporation officials estimate that they need at least Rs. 500 crores to perform this obligation. The share for capital works in the revenue expenditure of the SMC has gone up from 15.25 percent during 1971-81 to 23.55 percent in 1981-91 (Table 29). Returns from property tax, however, have declined. The city is generating civic assets, as is implied by the high rate of growth of capital expenditure. However, earnings from rents and fees from these assets have not increased in proportion, as is evident from their declining share in the corporation's revenue. The corporation has been able to increasingly depend on its own resources (Table 28).

TABLE 28

Share of Major Components in the Revenue Account of SMC during 1971-81 and 1981-91

(*in percentage*)

Component	1971-81	1981-91
Octroi	59.98	67.28
Property taxes	19.59	16.90
Rents and fees	5.69	2.76
Grants	12.72	7.69
Others	2.02	5.37
Total	100.00	100.00

Source: Compiled for SMC Budgets for different years.

On the expenditure side maintenance expenditure on water-supply, sewerage and storm water drainage together constitutes approximately 10 percent of total revenue expenditure. This has remained the same during the last two decades. As Table 29 shows expenditure on health and sanitation constitutes a comparatively larger share, which has increased slightly during the last decade, while primary education received a reduced share in the total. The share of "others", namely miscellaneous expenditures, has been found to be more than any individual item of expenditure. However, it has declined a little during 1981-91.

TABLE 29

Share of Major Components of Expenditure in the Revenue Expenditure Account of the SMC during 1971-81 and 1981-91

(in percentage)

Component	1971-81	1981-91
Water supply	7.85	7.24
Sewerage	3.02	2.36
Storm water drainage	1.34	0.54
Health and sanitation	15.48	17.94
Road	6.23	8.38
Public lighting	0.95	1.23
Primary education	10.23	7.83
Bridges and culverts	4.32	0.18
Finance charges	8.32	5.88
Share for capital works	15.25	23.55
Others	27.01	24.87
Total	100.00	100.00

Source: Compiled from SMC Budgets.

The revenue for capital expenditure usually comes from three different sources: i) spared revenue which is transferred to capital account, ii) from capital income arising out of sale of property, fixed assets etc., and iii) long-term loan from different sources. There is hardly any structural change in the composition of revenue in the capital account. Earning from capital assets constitutes less than 15 percent of total revenue. Despite significant transfer from the revenue account, a substantial portion of capital revenue consists of loans from the government and other institutional sources (Table 30).

TABLE 30
Components of Revenue in the Capital Account of SMC during 1971-81 and 1981-91

(*in percentage*)

Component	1971-81	1981-91
Transfer from revenue account	86.24	85.96
Income from capital assets	13.76	14.04
Total	100.00	100.00
Loan as % of capital revenue	25.32	23.95

Source: Compiled from SMC Budgets.

The share of water supply, sewerage and drainage has increased significantly in the capital account during 1981-91, as compared to the previous decade. The share of health related expenditure on civic assets has declined a little. The share of expenditure on roads, bridges and culverts has been significant, whereas that of fire service, street light and recreation centres has been very low. It is obligatory for all corporations of Gujarat to spend for provision of basic facilities for the area dominated by the Scheduled Castes, Scheduled Tribes and other backward classes. A certain percentage of revenue of the corporations are earmarked for that [Sec. 63(2), BPMC Act, 1979]. The proportion of expenditure towards SC/ST, which was as high as 18 percent during 1971-81, however, showed a significant decline during 1981-91.

TABLE 31

Components of Expenditure in the Capital Account of SMC during 1971-81 and 1981-91

(*in Percentage*)

Component	1971-81	1981-91
Water supply	3.49	14.18
Sewerage	4.85	11.47
Storm water drainage	1.30	6.73
Health and Sanitation	5.24	8.43
Road	17.59	14.25
Buildings	9.92	7.31
Public lighting	2.70	2.64
Bridges and culverts	10.82	12.98
Recreational centres	4.51	4.68
Fire service	4.62	2.64
Exp. for SC/ST	18.04	9.62
Others	16.92	5.37
Total	100.00	100.00

Source: Compiled from SMC Budgets.

The pattern of expenditure shows a clear inclination towards expansion of physical infrastructure vis-a-vis social infrastructure. Maintenance expenditure of physical infrastructure is found to be low as compared to that in social infrastructure. A significant portion of revenue surplus is used towards capital formation that has helped rapid industrialization in the city. Creation of physical infrastructure, however, has not helped human capital formation in the desirable way. In a city infested with environment-related diseases, it is only natural that expenditure on water supply and health will increase. In the capital account, significant change in this direction has been observed in the case of water supply, but the health sector has not gained much. In the revenue account, maintenance expenditure towards water supply has slightly declined while that of health and sanitation has increased a little.

TABLE 32
Share of Different Components of Revenue and Capital Expenditure of SMC during 1994-95 (Estimates)

Revenue expenditure		Capital expenditure	
Component	Per cent share	Component	Per cent share
Water supply	7.55	Water supply	17.40
Sewerage	2.50	Sewerage	5.19
Storm water drainage	0.46	Storm water drainage	3.47
Health and sanitation	19.12	Health and sanitation	4.90
Roads	9.80	Roads	14.74
Public lighting	1.38	Buildings	2.57
Primary education	0.18	Primary school building	3.00
Bridges and culverts	9.18	Public lighting	2.91
Finance charge	5.16	Bridges and culverts	10.68
Share for capital works	27.99	Recreational centres	4.47
Others	21.82	Fire service	1.54
		Vehicles and machinery	3.10
		Exp. for SC/ST	8.58
		Others	1.33
Total	100.00	Total	100.00

Source: Compiled from SMC Budgets.

The change in administrative structure from elected body to direct state administration has not been reflected in the financial pattern. This was only natural in the absence of an elected body when the SMC budget for the years 1994-95 was passed. The 1994-95 budget, therefore, reflected the same pattern as the previous budgets (Table 32). Maintenance expenditure on health takes the lion's share among the basic services, but asset creation in the health sector has been low. In contrast, asset creation for water supply services has always been the most important activity of the corporation. Expenditure on bridges and culverts and roads has, as usual, dominated the capital account. Capital formation on recreation centres has been almost as important as that on health and sanitation, while asset creation as well as maintenance expenditure on primary education has always been very low.

TABLE 33

Loan Status of SMC during 1989-92

(*in lakhs*)

Item	1989-90	1990-91	1991-92
Opening balance	1460.57	919.00	467.47
Income	297.63	300.00	580.00
Expenditure	839.20	751.53	768.59
Closing balance	919.00	467.47	278.88

Source: Compiled from SMC Budgets.

Besides transfer from revenue account for capital expenditure the SMC incurs substantial amount of loan from different sources.

It has been shown in Table 30 that expenditure financed by loan constitute 24 to 25 percent of total income in the capital account. But because of delay in decision making about projects and also delay in the implementation process such borrowed fund remains unutilised and carried forward to the next years account even though the corporation has to pay 5 to 6 percent as debt repayment charges. There is a large opening balance in the loan status of the corporation each year (Table 33). Because of the high opening balance carried forward from the previous year, the expenditure is more than the loan income every year in the corporation budget.

Financial Limitations

The city of Surat has experienced significant structural change in the economy. Establishment of large-scale industries, specially since the eighties, a plethora of small-scale industries, substantial increase in population through migration, large expansion of the city area and enormous growth of vehicles and shops have influenced the city structure in various ways.

These however, are not reflected in the budgetary activities of the local body. Financial exercise has mainly remained an income-expenditure account, without any capital budgeting taking the economic changes of the city into account. The city area has been doubled suddenly, making the corporation substantially rich in urban land, the most significant economic input. But the corporation's role has been confined to chasing people with basic services, thus always creating shortage of supply, as no thought was given to controlling demand. Physical planning has not been associated with capital budgeting in order to create the right kind of assets for the city.

The expansion of city area, specially towards the south, has brought many industries within the corporation boundary. It has increased the revenue of the corporation by way of octroi, as a majority of these industries (textile, diamond etc.) not only export the finished goods, but import raw materials also from outside the city boundary. It seems that gains through octroi are not sufficient to meet the liabilities as is evident from a shortage of basic facilities in these areas. The state government is empowered to decide on the expansion of city area, generally with the consent of the local body, which does not find it necessary to do any capital planning at this stage. Lack of assessment of municipal need and corresponding financial adjustment had led to severe shortage of basic services as the city size was expanded. Growing population brings in new electoral strength. So expansion of city area is generally hailed by the corporators. But perpetual shortage of amenities leads to continuous grievance which creates short term political gain for rival parties at the cost of the long-term city environment.

The corporation owns 42 percent of the total urban land. But it has not been able to make it sufficiently remunerative. The share of rent and fees in the revenue account has been very low and declining over time. Lots of building activities are taking place in the city pushing the land prices upwards. New sources of revenue should be explored in order to channelise these unearned gains of economic expansion to the corporation's advantage.

As a result, the city suffers from serious lacunae in financial management because of various factors, some of which are highlighted as follows:

i) lack of need-based and time bound programme,
ii) delay in implementation of various schemes resulting in price escalation,
iii) lack of perception on priorities between obligatory and discretionary duties,
iv) inability to collect taxes from some vulnerable areas,
v) inefficient tax-collecting machinery etc., and
vi) very low rates of taxes and charges.

It is not that the corporation did not do anything to provide basic services to the city population. It has completed quite a few major developmental works, the sources of which are worth mentioning. It has constructed a weir-cum-causeway at the cost of Rs. 40 crores. It has constructed major bridges on river Tapi to connect the western and eastern parts of the city at considerable expenditure on its own. It has also provided 15 developed plots for slum development for resettlement of the poor. However this has been far from adequate.

A part of the expenditure of SMC is set aside for areas dominated by SC/ST. The proportion of SC/ST population to total population in the city is not much, (4.34%) but in the slums, it is sufficiently high (15.7%). The corporation is following a policy of developing backward areas, generally dominated by the lower castes, but success has not been very impressive. The provision of dwelling units for the low income group is one of the obligatory duties of SMC, but the sweepers of the corporation are yet to get any accommodation. The meagre public residential units offered to these economically weaker sections proved to be much more expensive in real terms. These units are very far from their place of work and very inferior in quality. Instead of offering sub-standard houses, the corporation should consider, the possibility of offering easily accessible housing loans, which has actually been demanded by these groups.

The SMC is the second richest corporation among the six corporations of the state, but it does not have any significant commercial activity. The city which is the core industrial centre in whole of South Gujarat and a very prominent industrial centre in the state as well as in the country, has not been able to generate a significant revenue channel for the corporation apart from the traditional tax resources.

TABLE 34

Percentage of Recovery of Taxes against the Total Demand for all the Corporations and SMC during 1983-1989

Collection	1983-84	'84-85	'85-86	'86-87	'87-88	'88-89
Collection by SMC	50.98	51.03	50.44	57.33	35.54	69.69
Collection by all Corporations	44.15	48.13	40.06	54.71	47.27	38.11

Source: Gujarat Municipal Finance Board, 1991.

Note: Gujarat State has six Corporations - Ahmedabad, Bhavnagar, Jamnagar, Rajkot, Surat and Vadodara.

The resource position of SMC has always been comfortable as is evident from the increasing proportion of transfer from revenue to capital account. But this is only because of octroi collection due to industrial expansions. The corporation's own effort in resource mobilisation has been very limited. It has not exploited its existing sources also fully. The corporation has generally been able to collect only a little more than half of its total dues in taxes. The figures for the last decade show that the percentage of recovery has varied from 35.54 to 69.69 in different years (Table 34). However the performance of the SMC in this regard has been much better compared to other corporations in the state. The total collection of dues of all the corporations put together has been less than even 50 percent of the total dues on an average. Octroi collection by SMC is one and half times more than that by the corporation of Ahmedabad although the latter is two and half times big in area.

High earning of the SMC from octroi however, is not sufficient to cover the ever increasing expenditure in providing civic amenities. The property tax rates have not been raised since 1978. The elected local representatives are very reluctant to take any hard measures to raise local revenue. In the absence of an elected local body, the Administrator cannot take any decision as it is undemocratic. Hence demand for grants appears to be the only convenient as well as effective source of raising revenue. Recently, the corporation has placed its demands for consideration by the State Finance Commission.

The 74th Amendment has also left this issue untouched. The functions of the local body have been scheduled, subject to approval by the state, but the problems of raising internal resources continue to grow. In a growing urban centre like Surat, where land prices are rising by leaps and bounds, property tax rates are not much different from any other less prosperous urban area. There is no incentive for the local bodies for raising internal resources or economising on expenditure. In SMC, the revenue from property tax is tied to expenditure towards civic assets, (75% of the revenue should go towards capital formation) thus creating an impossible equation between stagnant resources and ever increasing expenses. Any step towards increasing internal resources through increased taxation is limited by political feasibility, more so, when the representatives and the voters live in close proximity with each other.

The SMC is obliged to provide to capital assets to the city, whereas in other states, this task is generally performed by para-statal agencies. For example, in Delhi, Delhi Development Authority constructs the physical assets of the capital and afterwards hands it over to the Municipal Corporation of Delhi for maintenance. In contrast, the role of the Surat Urban Development Authority has so far been confined to planning only. The 74th Constitutional Amendment Act has created more confusion regarding the role of these para-statal organisations (Jha 1993), thereby further complicating the corporation's tasks.

The urban local bodies have to take up the liabilities of urban growth which are generally preceded by changes in macro-economic policies. The industrial horizon of Surat began to change from the early 1960s but the local body did not undergo any visible change in the financial pattern so as to regulate the economic growth. In the USA, the local bodies can control residential density by charging different property tax rates in different areas within the city (Haynes 1991). In India, tax rates are not used for regulating urban growth. The 74th Amendment is also silent about this very important aspect of urbanization. The local bodies should be in a position to effectively direct the pattern of urban growth with fiscal tools as well. Assumptions of physical planning go haywire as physical control cannot suppress economic activities in areas which provide economic strength. Financial tools should be used not only to generate resources but to regulate urban growth as well. The 74th Constitutional Amendment Act hints at the possibility of more financial flow from higher authorities, but does not aim at strengthening the local bodies from within. As a result corporations like SMC are yet to be equipped enough to have an effective say in city management.

4. Corruption

The inadequacy of basic amenities in the city however cannot be entirely attributed to the lack of financial resources and lacunae in financial management. The present predicament of the city is the culmination of long neglect of basic amenities which has been the result of the predominance of self-interest and massive corruption in the SMC. This is the view of the common people, prominent citizens, officials, media and even some of the elected representatives as well. Though the media put the blame on officials selectively, they spared very few elected representatives when they said that cutting across political groups most of the elected representatives encouraged favouritism and nepotism. They said that both BJP and Congress were equally responsible for corrupting the Surat Municipal Corporation and its officials. Massive octroi evasion, illegal construction, rackets in tenders and bribery to name a few, continued jointly in full swing. So much so that a senior official alleged that in some cases the opposition party instead of resisting such moves colluded with the ruling party and sanctioned some projects which were not at all necessary for the city's development. Many of the corporators have a dubious background. A few of bootleggers, smugglers or criminals now own powerloom factories or dyeing houses to get a status of respectability in society. They constitute the new elite of the city, who participate in elections, sponsor public functions, float voluntary organisations and make donations to schools, hospitals and religious organisations (Shah 1994).

No political party can escape the blame of having perpetuated illegal encroachment. Excessive pressure of population has created scarcity of land in most of the cities in the country, which face the common problem of illegal and unauthorized encroachment by rich and poor alike. Big builders are violating all building bye-laws and constructing illegal structures, the poorer section is encroaching on government and municipal lands leading to excessive proliferation of slums and squatter settlements. Politicians do not take any steps against big builders in exchange for graft and do not resist the encroachment of government and municipal lands by the poor for fear of losing their precious votes. It is also alleged that some of the politicians are themselves involved in land grab and that they want to become corporators only to make a quick buck through illegal land deals.

When the elected representatives are themselves involved in such racketeering the officials have very little power to resist. Still the SMC during the last two years has been tough against illegal construction and in some cases has even demolished the illegal extensions in high rise buildings. In some unauthorized colonies it did not provide basic facilities like streetlights, water connection, drainage facilities etc.

Some of the officials also do not escape public accusation. It was alleged that a few officials have colluded with builders and political leaders and have become partners either to the big builders or estate brokers. Massive evasion of octroi is also alleged to thrive with the connivance of the officers with the traders.

It is however difficult to prove the allegations of corruption against politicians. A senior official expressed the view that if an official is dishonest he is always under scrutiny and is accountable to higher authorities but politicians are not accountable to anybody except to their voters who only can let them down.

5. Urban Governance and People's Participation

The role of city government undoubtedly is of utmost importance in effective urban management. But the effort of the civic body must be supplemented by meaningful public cooperation. Private entrepreneurs, informal sector service providers and owners of small-scale businesses, the non-governmental organisations (NGOs), the media, can all play a crucial role in urban development in their own ways. However public apathy towards city affairs has been highlighted by many as one of the contributory factors to the pathetic basic services condition in Surat. The public at large did not perform their roles properly.

Role of Industries

Industrial development in and around the city of Surat has been enormous during the last one decade. However the city government does not reap the benefit as much as it bears the burden resulting from such development. Instead, industrial development has created stresses and strains on the city infrastructure like roads, water supply, drainage system etc. Since most of the large units are located outside the city limits, the city does not get much revenue from them, except the collection from octroi. In exchange their contribution to the development of city infrastructure, both social and physical is almost negligible. In many other cities like Calcutta, Bombay, Delhi and even in the neighbouring city of Baroda or Vadodara the contribution of private establishments in infrastructure development, at least in the fields of education and health, is commendable. It is surprising that such ventures are almost absent in Surat.

Grievances against these industrial houses are many. The general complaint is that most of these entrepreneurs are not actual 'Surtis'. They are outsiders and have come to Surat only to earn money. They hardly have any local roots and do not have any sense of belonging to the city. At the first sight of trouble they are the ones to leave the city. They are no different from the huge migrant class who also have the same feeling towards the city.

The industry representatives however have different complaints. They allege that they are never consulted by the SMC while taking any decision which may affect them. As they are paying sufficient revenue in terms of octroi to the civic body they cannot take any further financial responsibility in the infrastructure development in the city. The contribution of industries to the state and central exchequer by way of sales tax, corporate tax, excise tax is nearly Rs. 500 crores per year. The city contributes a major share to the country's export earnings. They argue that the city government should get back from the state and central governments at least 10 percent of such revenues which they collect from the city for development of basic amenities. If they have to contribute to the infrastructure development they have to be given major tax concessions. They have also put their demand to the present Administrator for lowering the octroi rate which according to them is too high at present.

However the industries cannot avoid their responsibilities on this plea. Industry can help the local government in many ways. The urgent need is to cooperate with the SMC in making the city environment cleaner by not dumping their industrial wastes on the open ground or in the river. They should also help by providing their migrant employees at least basic shelter and health facilities. Though some of the industrialists are coming forward, such efforts are very few. One such effort is by the Surat based Waste Management Group formed by a young group of professionals and industrialists engaged in textiles. It is propagating the idea of bringing down hazardous chemicals in the textile industries by using their waste management techniques through which the textile mill owners not only create better environment but reap financial gains as well. Such efforts should be multiplied in the city.

Similar initiatives by industries in other cities can also be cited as examples which may be replicated in Surat. The Ahmedabad based National Sanitation and Environment Improvement Foundation formed by a prominent industrialist in the city has completed scores of sanitation and bio-gas projects and constructed public and private toilets on a 'pay and use' basis for Ahmedabad, Baroda and Bhavnagar Municipal Corporations. Surat Municipal Corporation has also invited the organisation to create 116 toilets in the slum areas of the city.

The example of Bombay First which has been formed recently in Bombay in line with London First for urban regeneration is worth noting. Launched by the Bombay Chamber of Commerce and Industry with an initial corpus fund of Rs. 25

million Bombay First aims to work jointly with representatives of the state and central government, NGOs, and a panel of experts to upgrade urban infrastructure like transport, housing, land use and civic services. It may not be an impossible proposition for the Southern Gujarat Chamber of Commerce and Industry to take such initiatives for the improvement of Surat city.

Role of NGOs

Effective urban management not only involves democratic decentralization and organisational coordination but it also needs involvement of citizens groups in the improvement of city services. Participation should come from non-governmental organizations (NGOs), the media, community based local groups etc. who should play a crucial role of a watch dog. They also channelise the demand for shelter, services and infrastructure to the local body. The NGOs help mobilise local resources, communicate information about needs to local political leaders, lobby for programmes and policies to expand urban services, provide financial assistance, promote new approaches to service delivery and interact with the municipal officials, programme managers and field staff (Rondinelli 1990). However the major weakness of the system of urban development in our country is the inadequacy of citizens' interaction through organised voluntary effort. Except selecting the representatives in the council once in every four or five years the citizens' participation in most of the cities is negligible. The present system is, therefore, neither truly democratic nor is it a presentative forum for projecting the needs of the people (NCU 1988). The common people or their representatives are either not consulted by the city government or they themselves remain aloof from the city affairs.

In Surat also quite a few non-governmental organizations are active, but except for creating public opinion their role in the field of basic services is not very visible. We contacted 8 prominent such organisations in the city for the present study, namely Kanjibhai Desai Samajshikshan Bhavan Trust, Sarwajanik Education Society, Navsarjan, Agha Khan Shia Imami Ismaili Council, Shri Surti Modh Vanik Samasta Pauck, All India Women's Conference, Surat Citizens' Council and Mahajan Trust.

Although almost all the above mentioned NGOs have shown their concern with the civic condition in the city, only five of them have reported that they are directly working for bringing an improvement in the civic amenities in the city. These organisations are - Shri Surti Modh Vanik Samasta Pauck, Agha Khan Shia Imami Ismaili Council, Navsarjan, Surat Citizens' Council, Kanjibhai Desai Samajshikshan Bhavan Trust. Chart 3 shows their activities in this regard.

Their interaction with the city government is not frequent and their role in communicating local problems and local needs to the officials is also minimum. Although seven NGOs have reported that the plague outbreak was due to the pathetic state of civic services in Surat, none of them had warned the SMC that the worsening civic condition could cause any type of serious calamity or epidemic if not plague. Therefore, so far as the apprehension of the plague outbreak is concerned, the NGOs and the SMC, were both completely taken aback. But the deterioration of civic amenities is not a new phenomenon. It is the outcome of long neglect. They failed to convey the timely warning to the local government. Unlike in the neighbouring cities of Ahmedabad and Baroda there is real dearth of organised voluntary effort in Surat in assisting the local government to solve the basic services problems.

The NGO representatives think that it is because of reluctance on the part of the SMC, to involve them in city development they cannot contribute significantly towards such efforts. They occasionally suggest various options for cooperation with the SMC but the suggestions are not taken in good spirit by the SMC. They have funds and they are eager to come forward but there is serious lack of initiative on the part of

CHART 3

Activities of NGOs in Improving Civic Condition in Surat

Shri Surti Modh Vanik Samasta Pauck	Agha Khan Shia Imami Ismaili Council	Navsarjan	Surat Citizens' Council	Kanjibhai Desai Trust Bhavan
Cultivate public opinion, help people with regard to public interest litigation against SMC and the state govt.	Create awareness regarding health and try to reach as far as possible to common public.	Take up urban health services, provide facilities like drinking water and toilets etc.	Make people aware of their duties, help people in redressing their grievances with regard to civic amenities.	Have adopted area housing, work for clean food preservation, provide nutritious food to children, child care facilities, dental health, education, etc.

the administration to work with them. They complain that SMC does not consider them as partners in the city's development and, therefore, does not keep in touch with them and contacts them only when the situation so demands. This fact was witnessed during the recent plague outbreak when SMC organised frequent meetings with the NGOs. In fact, when the plague havoc was at its peak, the SMC administration and voluntary bodies decided to urge doctors, who had left the city, to return. They even threatened to hand over a list of absconding doctors to the Medical Council of India recommending action against them. Besides, they also undertook a cleaning up drive in the city and cooperated with the SMC in its various curative and preventive steps.

To meet the crises emerging out of the plague all the NGOs rose to the occasion and tried to associate themselves for doing relief and rehabilitation work among the panicky people of the city. They particularly distributed meals, food packets and medicines among the affected people.

They also mobilised hundreds of trucks, excavators and loaders to clear garbage on a war footing. Within three-four days of the outbreak of the epidemic 47,000 tonnes of garbage were cleared using 50 loaders, trucks and excavators.

The NGOs blame the SMC for the precarious condition of basic services in the city. According to a majority of them, the elected body of the corporators does not help enhance the efficiency in functioning of the SMC. The elected representatives do not have any commitment to the people. They find that the style of functioning of the SMC remains the same whether there is an elected council or not. Some of the NGOs have even reported that they found the SMC in the worst style of functioning under the elected representatives. They have given the reasons for such a characteristic as the domination of anti-social elements involved in the municipal affairs, corruption, increased political interference, builders' mafia and warlords etc. create problems.

They feel, as the corporation officials are not interacting with the people they do not know about the people's problems. During the plague also SMC could not realise the gravity of the situation and it was not adequately equipped in terms of infrastructure to meet such a crisis effectively. Besides, some NGOs also feel that the SMC lacks coordination with other agencies and departments. This encourages some local people and persons with political greed to take the opportunity for getting publicity among the people. But all the NGOs are unanimous in their perception that the complete breakdown in civic services in Surat is the main reason that led to the insanitary conditions which in turn provided a breeding ground for the plague in the city for which SMC is primarily responsible. Besides, political inactivity and the lack of coordination with other agencies and departments etc. are some other reasons. According to them financial constraints are not any significant factor behind such a trend. Rather the prevalence of corruption in the SMC at various levels is the main problem. Inefficient revenue collection accompanied by the fact that a number of big industries do not contribute to the municipality by way of taxes and other duties in proportion to their income aggravate the problem.

To improve the civic facilities in Surat the NGOs are in favour of the involvement of the private sector in managing these services. They feel that if there is a private participation, there is an accountability. They also want that a monitoring authority comprised of the NGO representatives, prominent citizens, industry representatives etc. should be formed to keep a proper vigil on the activities of the SMC and it should be consulted in the decision making process. The officials however are skeptical about the NGO involvement in the decision making. According to them NGOs cannot be relied upon as a proper monitoring authority as they are either too good or they are easily purchasable.

Role of Media

The role of the media especially the local press is no less important in city affairs. By objective reporting they can create public opinion and public awareness. They can also expose both the city officials and elected representatives to public scrutiny for their misdoings.

Surat is a major centre of different types of Gujarati publications. This includes some of the prominent Gujarati dailies such as *Gujarat Samachar, Gujarat Times, Gujarat Mitra and Sandesh.* A high literacy rate and economic prosperity accompanied by people's general preference for the vernacular press has resulted in a wide circulation of Gujarati dailies in the city. Like other dailies, these newspapers also highlight the plight of the city's residents and the day-to-day problems which they face.

But the role of some of the local newspapers came under severe public scrutiny during the recent plague episode. A majority of the officials, corporators and common people expressed the view that because of the highly exaggerated reports by the local press Surat's image before the country and also before the world was tarnished. Instead of creating public awareness that plague is totally curable they actually fed the rumour. As a result people panicked and fled the city. It was alleged that this was not the first time the local press behaved so irresponsibly. During the riots in 1993, they published highly exaggerated death tolls, so much so that, to make the report more sensational they coloured the headlines in red. The prediction by a local *Jyotish* in July 1994 that the Ukai dam would break and the whole city would be under water also made headlines. The result was that nearly a quarter of the city population fled the city.

But this over-reaction of the press played some constructive role as well. Their reporting on day-to-day happenings during the plague not only helped the city administration, the state and national governments to come into action, and thus saved many lives, but it also brought into public notice the picture of urban environmental decay and lacunae in urban management. It exposed the national health policy. And most importantly, by measuring the impact of the epidemic for the first time in economic terms and not only by number of lives lost they brought to the notice of the government, planners and captains of industries that their capacity to create wealth depends not only on the infrastructure for power, communication and transport, but also on that which provides a clean and healthy urban environment like safe drinking water and basic sanitation. (David 1994).

The local press complain that despite their efforts in highlighting the local issues they have not been very successful in sensitising the SMC. Before the plague, some of the local press tried to give early warning in anticipation of a calamity as aftermath of the flood in their newspapers. The editor of the *Gujarat Samachar* informed us that his paper had discussed some of these issues in his newspaper in four main features when floods had occurred in the city in August 1994. This was just before the outbreak of plague in late September. The flood in August had resulted in the damage of 40,000 huts, 30,000 buildings and 4000 shops. Moreover, for at least four to five days bodies of dead animals continued to lie on the road. Although the possibility of the plague outbreak was not apprehended, the paper did express the possibility of an epidemic relating to some water-borne diseases. But in spite of these warnings the SMC did not launch any clean up drive in the flood hit areas, let alone the entire city. They squarely blame the city government as well as the state and central governments for the problems of the city.

The local press feels strongly that in spite of having adequate funds the SMC does not spend enough money on improving the drainage and sewerage in the city.

The high level officials of the SMC do not take due interest in ensuring the efficient delivery of civic amenities and public hygiene. In many cases there is an alleged collusion between officials and contractors which is promoting corruption and in the process the people suffer. Most importantly the concerned civic officials of the SMC lack a clear vision required for efficient delivery of civic amenities and administering the appropriate management of hygienic conditions in a rapidly growing city like Surat.

In such a situation the plague outbreak in Surat in 1994 put the SMC completely off-guard and put its machinery totally out of gear. Nearly 50 percent of the SMC vehicles were out of order. Although, the city is located on both sides of the river Tapi, SMC has only five boats which are certainly not enough to meet any calamity.

The shortcomings were more glaring in regard to sewerage and garbage disposal. When cleaning operations began in the city, there was no place to throw garbage while the drainage was already choked, making the entire cleaning drive of the SMC a mess. In this process two workers died and 200 were affected when garbage was being accumulated. The *Gujarat Samachar* has also reported that official figures of 69 deaths were far lower than the actual figures because many plague deaths took place in isolated areas outside the hospital which were not reported.

The press also feels that for the plight of Surat it is not only the SMC which is to be blamed. The state government has an indifferent attitude towards Surat. It does not pay due attention towards the planning and management of the city. Compared to the city's population and the gravity of various civic problems, the state government's grant to the city is very limited. While other cities such as Ahmedabad and Bharuch get more attention in the grant allocation, Surat continues to be neglected. Neither have the politicians who represent the city in the state legislature or in Parliament taken any interest in the city's affairs. They have failed to realise the infrastructural and civic shortcomings the city is facing in the wake of its intensive economic development in recent years which has attracted a large number of migrants resulting in tremendous population pressure on the city. According to them the neglect of local politicians is witnessed in other spheres also. For example, despite a large number of people going to Delhi or Bombay from Surat, the Rajdhani Express does not stop at Surat nor does the city fall in the major air routes of the country and there is no important air link available from here. People willing to use these facilities have to go to Baroda. In fact, the press people say that the air facilities in Baroda are used mostly by those coming from Surat.

Because of administrative and political deficiencies Surat's case for having better facilities remains unheard and an overwhelming majority of people continue to live with these ever increasing problems. The situation does not change much even if there is an elected body in the corporation. The local Surat press therefore, is probably not wrong in the apprehension that the plague epidemic may recur in the city in future also because its civic condition is again going back to the same stage where it was before the outbreak of the plague.

Workers' Unions

The general industrial climate in the city is not suitable enough for a successful worker's participation in the affairs of the city. The growth of small-scale unregistered producing units, the casual nature of jobs, inflow of in-migration outnumbering the permanent residents etc. do not provide sufficient ground towards the formation of strong workers' unions. There are some significant trade union activities in the textile sector, confined to the six large mills only. There are around 20,000-22,000 members in workers' unions in a city of nearly eight lakh workers. Two such unions are the Small Silk Mill Labour Union and the Dyeing, Bleaching and Finishing Worker's Union, they generally take up legal problems. There are four labour courts and one industrial court for handling workers problems. But an increasing number of pending cases and delayed judgements intensify, rather than solve the labourers' problems. The courts are not equipped with sufficient manpower, leading to an increasing number of pending cases, which are over 9000 at present. Sometimes, there is only one person in charge of all four labour courts. As long as these disputes are not settled, the workers cannot get their wages nor they can be absorbed elsewhere.

The industrial workers feel they are not properly represented in the SMC. Consequently, the problems surrounding their residential areas are overlooked. In any crisis like the spread of the killer disease, plague, they helped the community by taking the patients to the hospital and distributing medicines. The workers generally live in a very unhygienic environment, where any disease can spread any time. The workers themselves also do not take any kind of initiative to clean the surroundings.

Sudharai Mazdoor Union is another registered union formed by the sweepers of SMC. At present, there are 2600 sweepers on the pay-roll of the corporation. They are generally dissatisfied with the corporation's apathy towards their dwelling conditions. They do not have a housing society of their own. The very few public housing units offered to them are very far from their place of work and qualitatively much inferior compared to the price. The crisis that struck the city last year was very acute by nature. But within a short period, the administration rose to the occasion by supplying medicine, offering monetary incentives to the sweepers for more work etc. But it does not pay enough attention to the long-standing problem of malaria, which strikes every year. The acute drainage problem and congested living environment in the areas dominated by the economically weaker section make them vulnerable to any kind of infectious diseases.

CHAPTER V

Conclusion and Future Strategies

THE city of Surat which is situated at the Golden Corridor in Gujarat experienced remarkable industrial growth during the last one decade. This, while on the one hand has improved the employment opportunities and economic prosperity has also created scarcity for shelter, infrastructure and social services in the city. Excessive migration owing to industrial activities, frequent extension of city limits aggravated the scarcity of basic amenities. The city is now facing extreme congestion, air and water pollution and deteriorating public health services leading to frequent epidemics of various diseases every year culminating in the outbreak of plague in September 1994.

Our study was an endeavour to look into the factors responsible for the utter deterioration in basic services in general, which presumably led to the recent incidence of plague in the city.

Important findings of the study are as follows:

- At the physical settlement level the city is characterised by irrational land use disposition, inefficient land development and utilisation, shortage of housing, and related physical amenities like water, sanitation, garbage disposal etc. and large scale slums and squatter settlements and environmental degradation of varying degrees.

- The existing water supply system serves only 70 percent of the city population and 50 percent of its total area. The corporation water supply network is almost non-existent in the extended areas which came into its fold in the mid-eighties. Despite this the city water supply system utilises only half of its installed capacity and produces 200 million litres of water per day instead of 390 million litres.

- The sewerage system for disposing of liquid wastes covers only 30 percent of the population and 13 percent of the area. Waste water treatment facility is limited to half of the total water supplied. The other half is released in the river Tapti untreated.

- Piles of uncollected garbage on the streets and overflowing waste bins are a common sight. The city according to corporation estimates produces 1040 tonnes of refuse every day, of which 120 tonnes remain uncollected, although the corporation has 2500 sweepers on its pay roll to clean the city.

- The city roads especially those in the inner city area are extremely congested because of mixed land use pattern, narrow width of lanes and numerous bylanes. The 8 sq. km. area of the inner city has 14.4 percent road space while the city as a whole has only 4 percent of the area demarcated as roads.

- The narrow width of the lanes which were constructed ages back in the walled city area are not fit for an efficient public transport system. So the city bus service is almost rudimentary. Personal mode of transport is more dominant. The number of vehicles, especially the two wheelers has increased manifold during the last few years. According to the Central Road Research Institute (CRRI) while the total number of vehicles in the city increased by 13.5 times during 1968-69 to 1988-89, the number of two-wheelers increased by 38 times.

- More and more people are living in slums and in makeshift arrangements. Nearly one-third of the city population now lives in slums. During the last one decade while the total population of the city increased by nearly 66 percent the slum population increased by nearly 100 percent. The city area has extended and to that extent the slum population has also grown. Slums in the newly acquired industrial areas are deprived of minimum sanitation and potable water facilities. The level of services which was available in slums even twenty years back has now deteriorated to a great extent.

- The city suffers from extreme water and air pollution. Two principal sources contributing to the water pollution are domestic effluents and industrial wastes from thousands of small and medium dyeing, printing and other chemical industries. Sources of air pollution are the large industrial complexes in and around the city and increasing number of big and small vehicles.

- Because of the high level of water pollution every year the city suffers from various water-borne diseases, and sometimes they take epidemic proportions. It is said that in Surat there is a cyclical order of seasonal epidemics like malaria, typhoid, jaundice, diarrhoea and conjunctivitis every year from summer to the monsoon and the post-monsoon period.

- The health infrastructure in the city is utterly inadequate to cope with the problems. Population has grown at a tremendous pace but there has not been any proportionate growth in health amenities.

- It is observed that besides the factors like exceptional population growth, indiscriminate expansion of areas, technical and technological aspects related to specific service delivery systems and other factors like lack of people's participation etc., many of the distortions in the functions of the SMC at financial administrative and political level led to the precarious basic services conditions in the city. Financially the SMC is one of the most solvent local bodies in the country. In Gujarat, of all the six corporations the SMC has the highest per capita total income, which was on an average Rs. 771 during 1990-91 to 1992-93, whereas for major corporations like

Ahmedabad and Baroda it was Rs. 593.46 and Rs. 669 respectively. In the last two decades it has experienced approximately 190 percent increase in per capita revenue income and more than 400 percent increase in per capita capital receipt. But on the whole per capita capital receipt from different sources including loans from different external sources has remained very low.

- In Gujarat usually the maximum share of total revenue of any urban local body comes from its own sources, in the case of Surat it was nearly 96 percent during the last three years.

- Though substantial surplus from revenue account is transferred to the capital account each year and the corporation also takes loans from various sources for capital expenditure, because of the delay in decision making about a project and also delay in the implementation process such borrowed capital remains unutilised and carried forward to the next year's account. But the corporation has had to spend 5 to 6 percent of its revenue towards repayment of debt last year.

- The expansion of city area has brought many industries within the corporation boundary. It has increased the octroi revenue from 59.98 percent in 1971-81 to 67.28 percent during 1981-91. But this is the only buoyant revenue source for the corporation. Income from other tax sources is very low. Average return from property tax which was 19.59 percent in 1971-81 has come down to 16.9 percent during 1981-91. The low level of yields from property tax is hardly reflective of the dramatic escalation that has taken place over the last two decades in the real estate prices in the city. The property tax system continues to suffer from widely known problems of a narrow base, persistent undervaluation, low rates and poor enforcement.

- The corporation owns nearly 42 percent of the total urban

land in the city, but it has failed to make the urban land sufficiently remunerative. The share of rent and fees in revenue account has been abysmally low and is going down consistently.

- On the political front, prior to the 1995 elections for two years there was no elected body at the SMC. This further halted the decision making process. Except regular routine work, no major decision is being taken now as the local body is without an elected body. However, even when the elected body was there the representatives did not behave in a very responsive manner. During the last decade the city government faced extreme instability. The party in power changed almost every six months. Constant infighting between the ruling party and the opposition in the elected body hampered the day-to-day functioning of the SMC to a great extent, because change in the ruling party is invariably associated with shifts of emphasis in policy, delay in decision making etc. Therefore the political atmosphere of SMC during the last decade confirms that the mandate of the people certainly provides legitimacy to govern but it does not guarantee skill and wisdom.

- It is true that the effective city administration depends to a large extent on a strong city government which essentially means that democratically elected representatives manage the city affairs. As they are directly accountable to the people they take quick decisions in times of need. Governance by people's representatives increases the likelihood that development policies will reflect the local aspirations and priorities. However the present study reiterates that though the elected body at the local government is one of the most important prerequisites for successful urban governance, this is not a panacea for all its ills.

- Mere existence of an elected body is not sufficient safeguard against bureaucratization and delay in the decision making process. If that was so, the SMC which is luckier than many of its other counterparts in the country to face minimum supersession or cessation of governance by an elected body, would have performed much better and achieved greater success in providing services to the people according to their needs and priorities.

- In democracy there is no place for complacency. The occurrence of plague was not a sudden outburst in Surat. It was the culmination of long neglect on the part of the local body even under the democratically elected representatives which led to the deterioration in the service delivery system. Populist policies of the Congress ruled the corporation in the early eighties and massive expenditure in misdirected priorities during the BJP rule in the early nineties contributed to the precarious condition of basic amenities in the city. The political uncertainties arising out of several changes in the party equation in the corporation during the eighties jeopardised the continuity of policy and process of decision making. Rampant corruption among the elected representatives and officials, constant infighting severely damaged their credibility among the common people who are equally frustrated about elected representatives and officials.

- Some of the distortions in the urban governance, therefore, may be removed or reduced through decentralisation; greater vigilance by elected representatives may create more accountability among the officials and reduce bureaucratic hurdles and inefficiency but the democratically elected body is not an end, it is a means to achieve larger goal of effective urban management. The proper conduct of the governance based on actions and policies sanctioned by the people is of utmost importance.

- The study also establishes the fact that though a city or town cannot do without an economic base which creates employment for its inhabitants and also increases the income of the local authorities, economic development does not automatically improve the basic services and living conditions of a city, especially in those localities where a majority of the residents are poor. Therefore, there should be a conscious effort on the part of the local authority to provide basic amenities to its residents especially to the poor.

Future Strategies

To improve the functioning of the SMC in future for providing civic amenities to the city dwellers a few policy measures, many of which emerged during our discussion with different respondent groups, may be highlighted here:

1. For removing administrative deficiencies greater inter-agency and inter-departmental coordination is necessary. The coordination between the SMC and SUDA is of utmost importance as most of the urban chaos in the city has been attributed to the lack of perspective planning both within the city and its immediate neighbourhood. The SUDA is now in the process of preparing the new Master Plan for the years 2001-2021 for the city and its peripheral areas. The Master Plan should not be a mere bureaucratic exercise, which may create serious distortions later at the implementation stage.

2. As directed by the Parliamentary Committee which visited Surat after the plague, SMC should not take up any extravagant project until it covers all the neglected areas with the provision of basic amenities. Till then there should not be any further expansion of the city either.

3. Strict application of the Air and Pollution Control Acts should be observed by the Gujarat Pollution Control Board against the industries who are violating the norms by polluting the natural water body through continued discharge of hazardous and noxious effluents. Penal actions alone are not enough, more stringent legal actions, even

closure may be enforced if necessary. The offending industries in Surat at least now should be cautious after the recent Supreme Court order of 23rd March, 1995, directing the Central Pollution Control Board to issue notices to over 9000 small and large industries in and around Delhi for shifting to other areas within the National Capital Region, as they are vitiating the city environment by air and water pollution in total disregard of the Master Plan of Delhi.

4. For better financial management quite a few measures may be suggested:

i) The senior officials in the corporation suggest that existing tax rates need major upward revision. They suggested some new tax as well. Imposition of project related Capital Assets Creation Tax for 4 to 5 years is suggested by the Administrator of the SMC for creating infrastructure. The tax should be discontinued once the project is completed. Only a small surcharge can be imposed to meet the maintenance cost. However the project must be completed strictly within the specified time.

ii) Many of the respondents especially the corporators suggested better tax administration and collection, proper vigilance etc. instead of imposition of more taxes or increasing the rates.

iii) The state government should share more tax revenue with the local bodies. The grant from state government to SMC should be much more than the meagre sum it is getting now.

iv) Industries should cooperate in a much bigger way in developing city infrastructure. Some kind of development tax may be levied by the state government on the industries situated outside the city boundary. The proceeds can be shared with the local government especially for development of basic amenities.

v) An emerging theme in the study is the need to consider possibilities of an expanded role for private enterprise in the provision of infrastructure. The involvement of the private sector was suggested by almost all corporators and officials. Garbage disposal, construction of roads and bridges etc. are the services which are identified for private sector involvement. Private companies can construct roads, maintain them for a given period and collect tolls also. As a large number of heavy vehicles pass through the city roads, they need frequent maintenance which can be undertaken by the private companies.

The SMC can learn from such experiences in other cities. In garbage collection many corporations have undertaken the help of private companies and non-governmental organisations. For example, Excel Industries in Bombay takes a portion of the city's municipal waste and through scientific decomposition produces organic fertiliser. The Exnora International, a non-governmental organisation in Madras is doing excellent service in garbage disposal. Its organised manner of functioning and its role in overseeing public hygiene has been such a success that the concept of private participation in service delivery has now enthused the authorities in Bangalore, Vijayawada, Baroda, Pune and Bombay. Surat Municipal Corporation has initiated the effort and contacted Exnora International, but it is yet to start operating in the city.

The Rajkot Municipal Corporation has privatised the functions of preparation and serving of various municipal bills to the residents, maintenance of street lights, etc. Privatisation of conservancy services has also started since 1992. This has helped the corporation save the cost. Rajkot is the first city in Gujarat which has started levying toll tax on two bridges from September 1994. Private agencies are to be engaged for the tax collection.

The neighbouring state of Rajasthan has shown the way

by privatising octroi collection. Initially the scheme was to be operated in 27 out of 181 municipalities of the state. Now the scheme has been extended to other municipalities as well. Contractors have been appointed by these municipalities.

The SMC can also start such initiatives in a smaller way. But without a commitment on the part of the local government to impose significant and economically rational user charges private investors are unlikely to offer a viable solution to the infrastructure problem.

All privatisation efforts must be however under close supervision by the corporation. The corporation must have sufficient authority to cancel the contract on the indication of abuse of power by these private agencies.

5. The NGOs, citizens' groups and the city dwellers at large have greater obligation to help the authorities in keeping the city clean. The NGOs may create awareness among people about improving the habit. The residents in a locality must resist in a combined way the unauthorized encroachment and illegal construction activity in their area. In fact, some prominent NGOs can form a network to monitor the civic affairs in the cities.

The 74th Constitutional Amendment Act (1992) promotes the democracy at the local level and entrusts the elected representatives with decisive roles in planning, programme implementation and public service delivery. To perform these goals successfully the elected representatives and also the SMC officials need extensive training regarding their duties and responsibilities in the new environment.

However the above mentioned strategies will be successful only when the elected representatives give more importance to city development than their own personal interests. The elections to the SMC were held in 1995. Instead of adopting some populist policies, the new corporators must take concrete steps for clean environment, efficient system of water supPly and sanitation, leading to a more accountable and effective governance in the city.

APPENDIX

Responses of the Former Corporators

			Number
Corporators interviewed			15
	Male		13
	Female		2
Party affiliation			
	BJP		10
	Congress		3
	Janata Dal		1
	Independent		1
1.	Source of information about plague (more than one)		Responses (No.)
	i)	Local newspaper	9
	ii)	National newspaper	3
	iii)	Radio/TV	-
	iv)	Relatives/local residents/ friends	10
	v)	Doctor	2
2.	SMC's performance during plague		Responses (No.)
	i)	Satisfactory	5
	ii)	Not satisfactory	7
	iii)	Irresponsible	3
3.	Causes of unsatisfactory performances		Responses (No.)
	i)	SMC did not understand the gravity of the situation	6
	ii)	SMC is not equipped adequately for such emergency	2
	iii)	Lack of coordination between the central, state and local governments	7

			Responses (No.)
4.	SMC's performance would have been better if elected body were there		
		Yes	14
		No	1

			Responses (No.)
5.	Plague happened due to earlier negligence		
		Yes	10
		No	5

			Responses (No.)
6.	Causes of negligence (more than one)		
	i)	Administrative problems	12
	ii)	Financial inadequacy	10
	iii)	Political instability	4
	iv)	Lack of people's participation	10
	v)	Neglect of state government	12
	vi)	Irresponsible employees in the corporation	2

			Responses (No.)
7.	Causes of inadequate finance (more than one)		
	i)	Corruption in SMC	5
	ii)	Inadequate revenue collection	10
	iii)	Industry's contribution not sufficient	7
	iv)	Inadequate state grant	10

			Responses (No.)
8.	How to improve financial strength (more than one)		
	i)	Increase in rates of taxes and charges	4
	ii)	Better tax administration	10
	iii)	Levy more taxes	-
	iv)	Increasing grants	12
	v)	Scientific method of tax assessment	3

9. Support private sector involvement in provision of basic amenities	Responses (No.)
Yes	13
No	2

10. In which sector (more than one)	Responses (No.)
i) Garbage collection/disposal	9
ii) Drainage/Sewerage	3
iii) Water supply	3
iv) Road construction and maintenance	12

11. Is the postponement of Corporation election justified	Responses (No.)
Yes	2
No	13

12. Aware about 74th Constitutional Amendment Act	Responses (No.)
Yes	12
No	3

13. Would the recently amended BPMC Act endow more power to SMC	Responses (No.)
Yes	5
No	10

Bibliography

Census of India 1971, *General Population Tables - Gujarat.*

Census of India 1981, *General Population Tables - Gujarat.*

Census of India 1991a, *Provisional Population Totals, Rural-Urban Distribution.*

Census of India 1991b, Provisional Population Totals, *Workers and their Distribution.*

Census of India 1991c, *Primary Census Abstract - General Population*

Census of India 1991d, *Provisional Population Totals - Gujarat.*

Central Road Research Institute (1989), *Traffic Management Plan for Walled City,* Report, CRRI, New Delhi.

Das, Biswaroop (1994), *Socio-Economic Study of Slums in Surat City,* Centre for Social Studies, Surat.

Datta, Abhijit (1990), *Municipal Financial Management in India,* Report, Indian Institute of Public Administration, New Delhi.

David, L.H. (1994), 'Public Health Services', *Times of India,* October 12, New Delhi.

Fernandes, Allwyn (1994), 'Slow on the Uptake', *The Sunday Times of India,* October 9, New Delhi.

Government of Gujarat (1991), *Gazetteer of India - Gujarat State, Part III,* Gandhinagar.

Gupta, Rakesh, Gangadhar Jha and K.S.R.N. Sarma (1992), *Municipal Fiscal Stress - A Case Study of Financing Urban Development in Delhi - 2001,* Indian Institute of Public Administration, New Delhi.

Haynes, Douglas E. (1991), *Rhetoric and Ritual in Colonial India: The Shaping of a Public Culture in Surat City: 1852-1928,* University of California Press, Berkeley.

Hicks, Ursula K. (1961), *Development From Below,* Oxford University Press, London.

Hoshino, Claudia (1994), 'Land Development Process and Decentralisation in Latin American Cities and Metropolitan Areas: Issues, Trends and Prospects', *Regional Development Dialogue,* Vol.15, No. 2.

Jha, Gangadhar (1993) 'The Seventyfourth Constitutional Amendment and the Empowerment of Municipal Government - A Critique', *Urban India,* July - December, Vol XIII, No. 2.

Kashyap S.P. and R. S. Tiwari (1986), '*Shaping of Diamonds In Surat: Some Facets*', Sardar Patel Institute, Ahmedabad.

Mehta, Ashwin (1989), 'Suggestion for Improvement of Administrative set up of Surat Municipal Corporation', paper presented in the Seminar on Surat City Development, Southern Gujarat Chamber of Commerce and Industry, Surat.

Misra, R.K. (1994), 'Court to the Rescue', *Pioneer*, October 10, New Delhi.

National Commission on Urbanisation (1988), *Report Vol. II,* NCU, New Delhi.

National Institute of Public Finance and Policy (1994), The Implication of the Seventyfourth Constitution Amendment for the Finance of Municipalities, An Interim Assessment, NIPFP, New Delhi.

Pathak, H.N. (1984), *Diamond Trade and Industry in India*, Indian Institute of Management, Ahmedabad.

Philipose, Pamela (1994), 'Anatomy of a Crisis', *Indian Express (Magazine),* October 9, New Delhi.

Ramachandran, V.K. (1994), 'Filth and Decay', *Frontline,* Vol. II, No. 21.

Rao, N.R. (1985), *Municipal Finance In India,* Inter-India Publications, New Delhi.

Rondinelli, Dennis A. (1990), *Decentralising Urban Development Programmes,* Report, Research Triangle Institute, Washington.

Shah, Ghanshyam (1989), 'Slums and Development of the City', paper presented in the Seminar on Surat City Development, South Gujarat Chamber of Commerce and Industry, Surat.

Shah, Ghanshyam (1994), 'Economy and Civic Authority in Surat', *Economic and Political Weekly,* Vol. 29, No. 41.

Shah, P.C. (1989), 'Will Suratis'Remain thirsty in 21st Century?' Paper presented in the Seminar on Surat City Development, South Gujarat Chamber of Commerce and Industry, Surat.

Shiu, Evisoon (1994), 'Economic Analysis and Valuation of Urban Environmental Problems', *Regional Development Dialogue*, Vol. 15, No. 2.

South Gujarat University (1984), *Working and Living Conditions of Surat Textile Workers - A Survey*, South Gujarat University, Surat.

Stren, Richard (1994) 'Comment' on article 'Community Based Urban Environmental Management: Local NGOs as Catalysts' - by Yok Shiu F. Lee, *Regional Development Dialogue,* Vol. 15, No. 2.

Surat Urban Development Authority (1980), *Draft Development Plan–Surat Urban Development Area,* SUDA, Surat.

Tata Consulting Engineers (1994), *Surat Municipal Corporation Water Supply Master Plan* (Interim Report), Tata Consulting Engineers, Bombay.

Town and Country Planning Organisation (1985), *A Compendium on Indian Slums*, TCPO, New Delhi.

Webster, Douglas (1994), 'Managing the Urban Environment in ASEAN: The Case of Urban Regional Environmental Strategies', *Regional Development Dialogue*, Vol. 15, No. 2.

Index